How to Fall out of Love...
and Land on Your Feet

How to Fall out of *Love*...
and Land on Your Feet

Richard Silvestri, Ph.D.

and

Bryna Taubman

St. Martin's Press
New York

Design by Ellen R. Sasahara

Library of Congress Cataloging-in-Publication Data

Silvestri, Richard.
    How to fall out of love—and land on your feet / Richard
Silvestri and Bryna Taubman.
        p.   cm.
    ISBN 0-312-13088-0
    1. Love.   2. Interpersonal relations.   3. Interpersonal conflict.
4. Man-woman relationships.   5. Women—Psychology.
6. Self-esteem in women.   I. Taubman, Bryna.   II Title.
HQ801.3.S55   1995
306.7—dc20   95-7934
                                                                          CIP

First Edition: July 1995

10   9   8   7   6   5   4   3   2   1

Books are available in quantity for promotional or premium use. Write
to Director of Special Sales, St. Martin's Press, 175 Fifth Avenue, New
York, N.Y. 10010, for information on discounts and terms, or call
toll-free (800) 221-7945. In New York, call (212) 674-5151 (ext. 645).

To Sue, Kate, and Jillian,
whose love
and patient support
made this writing possible

✦ Contents

Contents

❥ Acknowledgments

$\mathcal{M}$Y DEEPEST APPRECIATION TO MY WIFE, SUSAN, AND my daughters, Kate and Jillian, for their love, encouragement, and enthusiastic support.

I would like to express my gratitude to my colleagues Drs. Harvey Milkman, Alan Schreiber, and W. Morton Feigenbaum for reading and commenting on the manuscript in progress.

I thank Oscar Collier, my agent, for years of support and encouragement; Ann McKay Thoroman and Ensley Eikenburg, my editors, for believing in this work and for their many invaluable suggestions and superb editorial guidance; and especially Lisa Collier Cool, who suggested I write this book, for her unique and creative ideas.

I am very grateful to Dr. Heywood Greenfield for the thoroughness of his review, comments, advice, and insights as a consultant to this work; to Jim Hudson for his advice and computer expertise; and to Stacey Ford for her all-purpose help with the preparation of the manuscript.

I also thank my therapy clients who have shared their experiences and contributed to my understanding of relationships.

There are many friends and family to whom I owe a special debt of gratitude for their generous help and support: Julia Cowles, Charles and Fran Dente, Gary Granger, Caren Greenwald, Anthony and Mary Silvestri, Judy Schreiber, and Chicky Greenfield.

I am truly grateful to Carol Levin Watson for her enthusiasm, insightful suggestions, editorial assistance, and typing of

Acknowledgments

the manuscript as well as for her continuing contributions as my publicity agent for this work.

I am particularly indebted to Bryna Taubman for her assistance and creativity in writing this book.

✦ Introduction

ENDINGS ARE ALWAYS HARD. THE DECISION TO END A relationship is one of the most difficult people face in a lifetime. Knowing when a love affair or marriage is over, telling a partner that you want out, starting a new life without a longtime companion—these are situations that bring anguish, uncertainty, and even grief to everyone involved.

This book provides a new approach to some of those decisions and help in understanding the problems that can develop. It is written for people who are in an unsatisfying, abusive, or troubled relationship but can't let go. It is also for those in a mismatched relationship, one that that provides little of the enjoyment and fulfillment of a good partnership. It is not intended for people who are going through a temporary difficult period in a relationship that is otherwise strong.

Many people eventually realize that ending a miserable relationship or marriage marks an important beginning. Facing up to the emotional adversity challenges them to change and mature, to take responsibility for their lives, and to make their own decisions.

This book explores all of the twists and obstacles on the road to that decision. It provides an understanding of how the mind works when faced with difficult choices and how best to make them. For example, rehashing a partner's flaws to underline your decision to break away may work against you. It can lower your self-esteem and feed your anger without providing an escape. Research shows that venting anger over unfairness only reinforces the feelings of rage and inequality. Losing control often makes you feel inadequate because nothing changes.

Instead of emphasizing what is wrong in your current relationship, it is more helpful to take steps to correct it, to change your situation so you can end the relationship and move on. To do that, you must examine why you are in the relationship. This means looking at the positives, not the negatives, so you know what is keeping you tied to a situation that makes you unhappy.

In this book I explain how it is that people remain in dead relationships thinking they can revive the past. I describe how focusing on a partner's flaws, using blame, is really avoiding the true motives that tie us to bad situations. And I offer suggestions on how to overcome fears of leaving. For many people, the sense of wasted years and the hope they can find a way to make that time worthwhile delays the decision to end a relationship. Others concentrate on changing a partner's impossible traits rather than on facing their own fear of leaving. Some people try to provoke the partner into making the break, often using subtle behavior—being excessively late or unreliable, for example. This may be effective, but it also can antagonize the other person, who may retaliate.

Some people are just bad partners. If you are involved with someone like that—the book provides detailed analyses of these personalities—it is important to recognize that you are not at fault. Good people can attract rogues, who see them as new opportunities to exploit or abuse. Rogues choose partners who avoid confrontation, who are willing to do all the work to make a relationship thrive, and who consider a commitment a promise and are reluctant to leave.

Besides detailing the personality types who offer the least hope of a lasting relationship, the book describes the most common forms of abuse and the most common responses to them. Many people involved with the types I call rogues or futile attractions consider their partner's traits unique and individual, a sign of their special qualities. Once they learn how predictable and calculating the partner is and see how those special traits follow a common pattern, they usually become much less enamored and are able to see the other person more clearly.

The book also provides some insight into why abusers act the way they do. Understanding that the behavior is part of the abuser's pattern and has nothing to do with what you did or didn't do can help a victim break free. Abusers are insecure; they can't believe that anyone can truly love them, so they try to dominate and control a partner. Your fear of leaving makes them feel powerful. That is why they humiliate and debase you, ridiculing any accomplishments or decisions that could lead to independence.

Case histories throughout the book offer insight and encouragement for those undergoing the difficult process of ending a relationship. Knowing how others broke free, learning of their successful escapes, and understanding how hopeless a continuing liason or marriage with an impossible partner can be can provide the motivation and confidence you need to make the break as well.

Two chapters describe in detail the twin signs of serious trouble: lying and infidelity. The stories of real people provide a background for analyzing your own situation and deciding if your partner's white lies and flings are momentary lapses or evidence of chronic problems. Other chapters help you learn the difference between care and control. We all like to think someone is worried about our health and safety, but a partner who insists on checking every movement, knowing every activity, and approving every contact with other people may be moving toward control and domination, not concern.

Unlike many other books, this one provides a realistic analysis of your situation rather than an automatic presumption that the relationship is fixable. If you are living with a sociopath, it doesn't matter how much you work to try to change his or her flaws. Love and communication cannot always overcome problems. Some people are just not salvageable, either because they don't want to change or because their traits are part of a personality type that is irreversible. That situation is beyond your control and your blame.

By explaining the nature and course of destructive relationships, this book shows how an attempt to make changes often backfires. Giving an ultimatum to an abusive partner probably won't work, but it is the only hope. Research has shown that standing up to abuse may encourage respect for you and turn the relationship around. If it does not, this book provides insight on how as well as why you should leave.

The book begins with discussions of destructive partners and relationships, exploring the personality types and situations that are hopeless. The second section explores the problems in and obstacles to taking the next step. It explains why indecisiveness is part of the process and how even depression helps you make a difficult, life-changing choice. By understanding these processes, they become less frightening and provide you with more control as you experience them.

The second section also explores the guilt and anger that develop in the wake of a failed relationship. In most cases, the guilt can be alleviated by seeing clearly how a partner's personality made the relationship hopeless. Finally, I discuss what may have caused you to enter into a partnership with someone so unsuited. By recognizing a pattern, you will be able to understand how your own anxieties or insecurities contributed to your choice; then you can make a better decision the next time.

This book provides information that will help you fall out of love, overcome your fears and depression, recognize the patterns and characteristics of bad relationships with rogues and futile attractions, understand the patterns in your life, and make corrections if necessary, and then move on. It explains how the mind works to heal itself, so you can help, not impede, the process. By reading how others have overcome similar problems and learning to identify telltale signs of a bad relationship, you can learn to avoid making another mistake. Instead, with effort and understanding, you can find your way to a loving, fulfilling relationship with a partner who provides the support, companionship, and trust we all long for.

❥ 1

Are You Ready to Let Go?

Should i stay in this relationship?"
In one form or another, that's the question most of the psychologists I know hear most often in therapy. Men and women feel trapped in relationships; they also feel guilty, anxious, or embarrassed about ending them.

Frannie, an attractive twenty-six-year-old editorial assistant, looked nervously around my office and lowered her voice to a whisper before saying the words that she considered a betrayal of her second husband. "I married him on the rebound. He's a nice guy. Maybe too nice. But not for me. My first husband was abusive, and I guess I overreacted. This marriage is a mistake and I want out. How can I tell him?"

Barbara is forty-six and wants to get married. Her current boyfriend, Ken, is an engineer who really cares about her. She likes him, maybe even loves him, but she hates the two packs of cigarettes he smokes every day and the six-pack of beer he drinks every night. He promises to change but never seems to try. She doesn't know what to do: Learn to live with his bad habits, try to change him, or look elsewhere.

Jack thought he and Jane had a good marriage. They had two small children, and both worked hard. He was developing a cleaning business and often put in sixty hours per week. She sold real estate. Then she had an affair with a man she met at work. Jane said her marriage seemed hollow and Jack invested more time in his business than his family. She broke off the affair, but Jack didn't think he could ever trust her again. He also felt humiliated and angry and wasn't sure he could overcome those feelings to save the marriage.

Celia never knows if her husband will come home pleasant or turn vicious and insulting. His mood swings make her insecure, but she is dependent on him financially. Although she has no outside income, she dreams more and more often about escaping his abuse. The longer she delays making a decision, the more difficult leaving seems to be.

Countless women and men face this agonizing uncertainty. Since we all value commitment—feeling loved and wanted by someone we respect and desire is a big piece of our sense of self-esteem—we're usually very reluctant to end a relationship, even one that's turned sour.

If we're in a marriage or affair that has undoubtedly spoiled—such as Frannie's marriage to a man she no longer respects or admires—we often cling to the remains, hoping to find a solution that spares us the guilt, the risks, and the pain of parting.

Financial advisers say holding a stock on the downside is a losing proposition. It's best to cut your losses, admit a mistake, and sell. Then you can find a stock that's gaining. When love turns to apathy, the sooner both sides acknowledge the end, the quicker they can both move on to something and someone better.

People often refuse to let go, unable to acknowledge that the love they once shared is irrevocably gone. Instead, they grasp eagerly at any sign of hope.

Many of us remain in empty, unhappy, or barren relationships out of fear. We're afraid that the misery of leaving will be even worse than the agony of staying. The door to freedom opens onto a dark, unpredictable world. The unknown holds surprises and is often more terrifying than the world we know.

Change is always uncertain, but being in a toxic love affair poisons our outlook, adding a veil of gloom over the future. Happiness seems like a distant memory and serenity an impossible fantasy. Anxious and unhappy in our current relationship, it is difficult to imagine feeling passionate about someone new or even just reveling in solitude and privacy. When the men and women I work with summon the courage to break off a bad relationship, all say their main regret is not acting sooner.

Janet, a forty-two-year-old CPA, wanted a serious, committed relationship, but her married lover refused to leave his wife as he had promised. She considered their affair hopeless, but he kept begging her to be patient. It took her months to dump him, but once she did, she grudgingly acknowledged that "Sometimes, nothing really is better than something."

Janet and Frannie are among the hundreds of people who have learned techniques that helped them to face their problems objectively and then make unemotional, informed decisions. By using the strategies described in the following chapters, you, too, can learn ways to make the necessary decisions in your personal life. They will help you over what seem to be insurmountable obstacles to a more hopeful future.

Relationships often fail. Half of all marriages in this country end in divorce, and most love affairs that don't result in marriage come to an end. American society no longer stigmatizes couples who split up. It is much healthier to bury a dead relationship than to live, like Norman Bates in *Psycho,* with the mummified remains.

Ending a long-term relationship, whether a marriage or a love affair, is a major life decision. Breaking up evokes anxiety, guilt, anger, frustration, disappointment, doubt, uncertainty, sadness, and dozens of other negative emotions even if you do it for all the right reasons. You are breaking a promise, ending a serious commitment, changing everything about the way you have been living, maybe ending a family. These are not actions, or decisions, to be taken lightly.

How can you tell if something else will be better? Are there lights to guide you through the darkness, clues to help you make a decision? How can you be sure divorce is the answer?

Is there a chance to save your relationship? Is there hope your lover will return? Is there any possibility your partner will make a permanent commitment? There are signs, not always the most obvious ones, that indicate if a marriage or affair is DOA or just needs some time in the ICU.

If you're not sure what to do, read the following statements carefully. Do some of them sound familiar? Do you recognize your partner? Can you find reflections of your own experience? If they describe your life recently, you are ready to give some serious thought to your next step.

• **Thoughts of leaving, or being left, pop up constantly, even when you try to think about something else.**
Through evolution, the human brain has developed a survival technique that demands we pay attention to threats. Any negative feeling—one that is distracting, depressing, anxiety producing—is a threat to survival. A trivial psychological threat—an inadvertent insult from a stranger, for example—may catch our attention briefly, then be replaced by more important concerns.

The loss of our most important relationship is a much more dangerous threat. No matter how much we may want to avoid the pain of contemplating such a threat, the mind returns to it again and again whenever we aren't actively suppressing those thoughts with distractions. We find ourselves thinking about the relationship and the future even when we are trying to concentrate on work, balance the checkbook, or cook dinner.

The more you try to distract yourself from the troubling thoughts, the more frequently and fiercely they will flare up later. Psychologists call the attempted distraction a "flight to activity." But it provides only temporary relief. It's as though your mind was sending you a signal. You may be trying to ignore the problems in your relationship, hoping they will disappear, but deep down you recognize how serious, and threatening, those problems really are.

• **You have sudden and unexplained aches and pains, or
other minor physical symptoms.**
Often the pain of being in a bad relationship is physical as
well as emotional. Men and women in troubled love affairs
may experience rapid heartbeat and breathing, dryness of the
mouth, neck or shoulder pain, headaches, tensed muscles in
the back, gastrointestinal problems, or frequent urination.

Many of these complaints are caused by another early
human survival strategy—the powerful "fight-or-flight" reaction. The tensions of being in a hostile, hopeless love affair
come across as a physical threat, and the body responds to
psychological stress as it would to a potentially lethal physical
assault.

Failing to respond to the threat makes the symptoms
worse, just as someone will yell if you ignore a spoken warning of oncoming danger. When the body feels threatened, it
releases chemicals—adrenaline, among others—to help organize a response and find a way to neutralize the threat. Since
most threats to early humans were physical, the simplest response was either to attack or run away: fight or flight.

Today, the threat is just as likely to be emotional or psychological, but the same chemicals are released. If we don't
act, the potent chemicals reverse their effect; physical
strength, coordination, and vitality decline, making us feel
run-down and susceptible to illness.

According to some studies, emotional stress either causes or
aggravates three-quarters of the problems that result in visits to
a physician. If you can learn to reduce the emotional stress in
your life or at least make an appropriate response to the fight-
or-flight chemicals, you will be a lot healthier and happier.

• **Your behavior has changed, and not for the better.**
Behavior changes are as varied as humanity itself. You may
find yourself unusually short-tempered with friends, coworkers, or even the clerk at a supermarket. Other signs that romantic worries are affecting your life include giving up

activities that you used to enjoy, neglecting crucial chores, crying or flying into a rage about minor criticisms or frustration, and having problems concentrating on crucial tasks.

These symptoms are also signs of depression. Recognizing them can mean that your anxieties about the relationship are so great that you are beginning to despair about finding a solution. Other signs of trouble are emotional or physical withdrawal, loss of ambition, a preoccupied or distracted attitude that leads to mistakes and injuries, indecisiveness, forgetting things, difficulty working, and increased awareness of other potential partners.

• Nothing your partner does pleases you, and you often do or say something you know will provoke anger.
People who want to end a relationship often act obnoxiously. Reluctant to hurt their partner or fearing an emotional scene, they hope the other person will get disgusted and take action first. Psychologists call this passive-aggressive manipulation. Those who use it may find it gratifying to vent their frustration and rage with subtle, but hostile, behavior while denying any intentional harm.

Stuart fell out of love with his domineering wife, Abby, years ago but couldn't bring himself to ask for a divorce. Instead, he changed his previously accommodating behavior. He came home later and later, insisting he needed the overtime to pay Abby's bills. Then he began to act erratically: One day he'd find endless ways to provoke her, the next he'd be affectionate and contrite. When Abby suggested marital therapy, Stuart agreed, then used the sessions as an opportunity to vilify her. Eventually, he got his wish. Abby got fed up and hired a divorce lawyer.

This tactic is often used by people who are sensitive and kind in an attempt to prepare the mate for the impending split as well as to enlist his or her support. You may think you're being kind, but the result in most cases is usually far crueler than making a clean, honest break. Even if the love affair is a lost cause, there is no advantage to antagonizing your mate, and by making a clean break you can maintain your self-respect and sense of fairness.

• **Your memories of the major events in the relationship have changed significantly.**
Current disappointment can make it difficult to remember happier times together. Some people revise history, seeing evil motives in things that once seemed endearing.

When they were courting, Sally was thrilled by Bob's attentive behavior. She saw it as proof of his love. After she'd grown disenchanted with their marriage, she thought of it as a manipulative strategy to control her and keep her in the relationship.

Revisionism isn't necessarily fatal to a romance, but it's an ominous sign. You're looking for clues from the past to explain your present predicament. Finding them may increase internal tension, however, because the loving actions then are out of sync with your hostile feelings. Some people try to eliminate this disturbing inconsistency, often thinking that if they ever loved the person, it was because they were tricked. The good old days weren't actually any good at all.

Intensive care can revive a romance even this far gone. At least you're still searching for positive things. Sally and Bob came in for counseling and eventually worked things out. Her memories regained their former luster and she again delights in remembering her husband's extravagant attentiveness when they first dated.

If, on the other hand, your memories are not revisionism, but reality, then seeing them clearly may be a crucial first step toward falling out of love with the wrong person.

• **You—or your partner—have made an important change in lifestyle without consulting the other person.**
Very often, those who are seriously contemplating the end of a love affair experiment with different lifestyles, for example,

finding new friends who don't see them as half of a couple or taking up activities and interests their partner doesn't share. They may also change attitudes, habits, or appearance.

Suzanne was forty-two and married to a very successful business executive. She suddenly developed an interest in aerobics and began exercising every day, spending hours at the health spa. She made new friends there, got a new haircut, and changed her style of dressing. Shortly after she was certified as an aerobics instructor, she told her husband she was moving out. For years, she had known about his affairs but felt too trapped in the marriage to raise the subject. Once she found a life of her own, she was free to take action.

Martha stopped working on the house and garden with her husband on weekends. Instead, she went to church with friends. She changed her dress and attitudes to match, buying more conservative clothes and finding fault with Mike's drinking buddies. Voicing her disapproval of Mike's excessive drinking and lack of respect for her, it wasn't long before Martha was on her own and spending her evenings with her church group.

When one person in a relationship stops thinking about feelings of dissatisfaction and starts acting on them, the future of the couple is dim. Unilateral decisions that mean major changes in the way the household operates are sure signs of new directions. If half of a pair gets religion, starts a heavy exercise regimen, changes appearance, or abandons home cooking for restaurant meals, the partner may have reason to be concerned.

• **You fight a lot, and always about the same thing.**
This may not be as bad as it seems. When you engage in battle, you're still trying to work out your disagreement. Fighting reveals that some life is left in the love affair. Arguments on one topic suggest that you believe change for the better is not only possible but also worth fighting for.

It may seem paradoxical, but arguments are a powerful

indication that you truly care for your partner. Why else would you consider what he or she thinks or does important enough to argue about? This symptom is often an indication that the relationship can be saved, if you act immediately on it.

Frequently the real problem isn't what you fight about, but how you fight. Instead of resolving disputes, the arguments perpetuate them. You've slipped into a vicious cycle with both of you focused on proving you're right and neither stopping to examine the basic discontents at the bottom of the conflict.

Eileen hears Steve complaining about her late hours and is convinced he's too selfish to be supportive of her career. He protests her long and frequent business meetings, sure she's neglecting their marriage because she doesn't love him anymore. Since they're deaf to each other, a counselor could help them break the pattern of unproductive arguments and find a compromise. Once each starts really hearing what the other is saying, Eileen and Steve may save their marriage.

It's worse when the arguing stops; that means you have given up on the relationship. This is a sign of defeat. Neither partner cares enough to fight. Convinced nothing will change, they view the relationship as a lost cause.

Toby is forty-four. She and Sam have a functional relationship after twenty years, but not much more. They rarely fight. They rarely speak. They've developed their own interests and friends and meet only for family meals. Their youngest child is almost ready for college and Toby is thinking about leaving at the same time, sure there must be something else.

• You're having an affair or you suspect that your mate is.
Even this most primal betrayal is not necessarily the death knell for a romance. Some affairs are a selfish, but temporary, indulgence when people think of their life as drab or depressing. The reasons may have little to do with their mate and

instead stem from frustration over a dead-end career situation, a medical condition, or financial problems.

By keeping the comforting security of their marriage while enjoying the guilty pleasure of a secret love and novel sexual adventures, they hope to add to what they already have. Studies confirm that it's relatively rare for people to end a marriage because of an affair. More than 75 percent of the time, the cheating partner opts to stay with his or her spouse.

If infidelity is the problem in your relationship, understanding why it happened helps in the next decision, to forgive or not. If the cheating was an impulsive interlude during some depressive episode in your partner's life, the odds are you will be able to rebuild your relationship, *if* you really want to. But if infidelity is one of many moves the other person has made away from you, the prognosis for a happy future together is poor.

• You're sure you want to leave, but you keep changing your mind.
Your mind wants immediate action to end this pain, but your heart knows that pain is inevitable regardless of what you do. As soon as you settle on one choice, you remember the advantages of the other solution. You swing back and forth, trying to hold on to both. This indecision often strikes when you have to choose between alternatives that are not comparable, such as the best interest of your children versus your own personal happiness.

The anxiety produced by your indecision may lead you to doubt your ability to choose. You wonder why you just can't make a decision and stick with it. But what seems like indecision may also be the best way to make the right decision. Just as Americans soon became enured to pictures of Somalis suffering from famine, repeatedly confronting disturbing emotions gradually blunts their sting. Once you are free of emotional pain, you can weigh the merits of the relationship more calmly and rationally.

• You talk to someone about leaving.
Open discussion, even if only to a trusted friend or a therapist, brings a decision closer. Probably, you've spent months mulling over the alternatives and now you want to test your reasoning. Most of us choose someone who's objective about the romantic situation but apt to be sympathetic to our views. A frank discussion may be a step toward lining up a potential support system for yourself before you actually make the break. Talking it out with someone can also provide a rehearsal, a way to practice approaches before you confront your partner. It is important to realize that if you discuss dissatisfactions with your partner to a friend, you may unwittingly destroy any positive feelings that existed between the friend and your partner. This can be a real problem if you decide to reconcile and can even cost a friendship.

• Your partner is demanding more space or time to be alone or with friends.
Neither of the two most common reasons for wanting more space bodes well for your future together. The first is simply that the space your lover wants is found in the arms of someone else. As noted, that may be temporary, but infidelities force both of you to examine what the partnership lacks. Another possibility is that your lover wants to be alone to explore life as a single person. What starts as a parallel life often evolves into a separate life, making the actual break or divorce a formality.

Those who ask for more space usually feel conflicted and guilty about their need for separation. This can increase the intensity of the need as the confused partner tries to escape from the person evoking the guilt. Sometimes, developing new shared interests and showing flexibility can save the relationship. But the demand for privacy is a serious omen; trying to tighten ties to a restless partner can precipitate a final break.

16

• **You keep secrets from your partner, no longer sharing even trivial joys or passing thoughts.**
Knowledge is power. Sharing, even things that bring pleasure, makes us vulnerable. When the end is near, you protect yourself from any weakness, and one way to guard against emotional risks is not to reveal anything about the inner self. Even sharing seemingly insignificant things—an amusing thought while reading the newspaper or a petty annoyance at work—may accidentally hand the other person a psychological weapon to use later. At best, it creates new bonds with someone we are trying to break loose from. Better, and safer, to keep one's thoughts private.

Some couples stop talking because the partner considering separation fears that any conversation will inevitably lead to a premature discussion. Revealing small secrets could pave the way to blurting out the big one—this relationship is over. For people not yet ready to break this devastating news, it seems safer to stay silent about any personal topic. Such an emotional withdrawal is an early sign of trouble.

• **The thrill of sex is gone.**
Sometimes the negative feelings we refuse to acknowledge aloud come out in other ways. Physical attraction may be the first link to snap in the chain that forges a partnership.

A loss of erotic interest may have a chemical explanation. When the stress of unresolved hostility activates the potent fight-or-flight response, the body is roused to face possibly life-threatening danger, not prolonged bouts of eroticism.

The end of lust may also be psychological. When a relationship is working, arguments often end in bed. But when the ties are fraying, making love may end the battle but not eliminate the cause of the war. The partner who is still angry feels betrayed, forced into denying strong feelings.

For those secretly considering a separation, intimacy may be even more difficult. A lack of physical attraction may be a warning signal—the two of you simply don't fit together anymore. People frequently send mixed sexual messages when thoughts and actions haven't caught up with instincts.

After years of marriage, Ellie refused to indulge her husband's sexual fantasies. She was willing to cooperate in the standard positions, but that wasn't enough for Frank. In their mid-forties and both professionals, her decision marked a turning point in their marriage. In therapy, she complained that he worked too much and ignored her. She felt he didn't care about her and showed her no respect. Frank was amazed and angry when she changed their sexual pattern. He argued that she didn't appreciate how little he asked of her. After some discussions, Frank realized that in order for Ellie to feel comfortable and willing to please him, she had to feel that he truly cared about her, not just that he was a good provider.

Anger, anxiety and insecurity about the relationship are the most common reasons for a sudden change in sexuality or frequency. Intimacy is an important part of a good relationship, and occasional diversions from the norm are a sign of continued eroticism and spontaneity. But a persistent decline in interest may signal serious problems.

• **You chiefly value your partner for the high he or she gives you.**
During the initial euphoria of a new romance, it's hard to tell whether you're in love with the other person or simply in love with love.

Infatuation is passion, not love, and arousal alone, no matter how exciting, isn't enough to sustain a committed relationship. After the thrills of responding to a new lover and sharing secrets lose their piquancy, we crave something deeper and richer to nourish our heart and spirit. When we're in love, we worry about our partner and how he or she feels. If your biggest concern is how good your partner makes you feel, a reevaluation may be in order.

Angie, for example, doesn't miss Tony since their breakup.

But she does miss his attentions to her—the three calls a day to ask about every trifling detail of her life, the exquisitely thoughtful gifts, and the extravagant compliments for everything she said or did. Angie never cared about Tony's guilt over being involved in an affair. And she rarely expresses any interest in how he is getting along now, a sure sign that she was hooked on the arousal of illicit sex, not Tony.

Love means caring for the beloved, sharing trust, and an emotional attachment as well as responsibility. It starts with passion, then deepens into concern, satisfaction, and reliance, but not total dependency. Both partners make long-range plans, sharing a vision and a commitment to each other and the future together. The morning after brings peace and contentment. With love, you want to meet your partner's needs and he or she wants to meet yours.

By contrast, lust is arousal, followed by withdrawal. It is like other addictions, characterized by how it makes you feel right now. There may be short-term planning—a vacation or restaurant—but time reveals flaws, and boredom often means escape. Infatuation, or lust, concentrates on your needs alone—for sexual climax, for social status, for financial gain, for physical attraction—and how your lover fulfills them. Without long-term respect, liking, concern, and commitment, the intensity of early passion burns itself out.

• **The relationship is empty.**
Your partner no longer satisfies important needs like intimacy, trust, or commitment. The thrill is gone and nothing takes its place. Once the gloss of newness wears off, cute habits become annoying mannerisms and those shared activities become boring chores. You two have nothing in common and can't seem to find anything to do together, not even sex.

George works hard. During the week, he's at his automotive business, then stops at the gym. On weekends, he teaches skiing. He comes home late and exhausted seven nights a week, and his wife, Belinda, feels abandoned. They've talked about it, but nothing changes. She is a teacher and has her own friends. She's also having an affair. Belinda knows the marriage is over, but because of financial worries she is anxious and uncertain about getting a divorce.

Your relationship has reached bottom when you no longer feel any emotional attachment to your partner. It's not just that you no longer love the other person, you don't feel anything at all, not even anger. Emotional and physical withdrawal, absence of shared interests and activities, even a lack of arguments are all signs that this marriage or affair is played out. Neither one of you cares enough about the other to make an effort or evoke a response.

It can be hard to leave even an empty relationship, however. Any partnership develops habits of responding to needs over time. You may not be getting enough intimacy, trust, affection, attention, respect, or whatever from your partner, but you can't be sure anyone else will meet those needs either. That uncertainty makes it difficult to move on despite the current unhappiness. Many people are too dependent on a partner for what he or she does provide to start looking for something that may not exist.

• **If your lover decided to leave, you would break out the champagne.**
You don't want to be the one to say it's over, but if your partner took action, you wouldn't mind at all. Initiating a breakup is a significant decision, and most of us would rather someone else shoulder the burden. This daydream represents a guilt-free solution to a major problem, a decision made without agonizing, action taken without pain to anyone. Like most fantasies, it's unlikely to happen. If you are daydreaming about how to celebrate your lover's good-bye, then you should examine your fears and reasons for staying and prepare yourself to move on.

Certainly not all of the above exactly describe your situation. We bring unique experiences, needs, and intelligence to our personal situations. But if one or more of the statements sound familiar, evoke a nod of recognition, or initiate a new train of thinking, the chances are you're already looking for an escape hatch.

The decision to stick it out or get out is one only you can make. Ultimately, any threat to your comfort, peace, or survival demands a fight-or-flight response. But there are techniques, methods, and strategies that provide weapons for the fight and a road map for the flight. These techniques are described in detail in later chapters, but the following list provides an outline of your defenses:

- Concentrate on your own growth, not on the relationship. Look for ways to expand your horizons professionally or personally. Test new interests, explore new places, make new friends.

- Learn to desensitize your anger and your fear of change and loss. Feelings of hurt, blame, guilt, shame, and failure are also dangerous obstacles. You can control and dilute their effects and overcome their traps.

- Changing your personal circumstances has a ripple effect. "Wife" conjures up one stereotype; "single parent" or "divorcee" an entirely different image. Other people may respond differently to you, and your own self-image may change as well. It helps to be prepared for your new impression.

- There often are immediate benefits to making a separation. You are free to pursue your own priorities and interests. You can focus on your own needs without being concerned about your partner's demands. Many people become more assertive, learning to depend on themselves. Repeated successful experiences solving problems for oneself enhance self-esteem.

➤ Try to anticipate and solve conflicts about custody, visitation, and property ahead of time and without bitterness. Especially when children are involved, it is important to maintain communication with your partner. Provoking rage may make it easier to leave in the short run, but over time, that anger can destroy any hope of a reasonable settlement and harm your children. Determining who is morally right is not that important when it colors your children's views of family.

➤ You need a new support system. You can no longer expect your partner to meet your needs, emotional or financial. Family and friends can help with psychological support, but money is probably beyond them. Be prepared for reduced finances until things are settled and you can work out alternatives.

♪ 2

Magnificent Illusions

𝕸AGICIANS CREATE ILLUSIONS TO ACCOMPLISH their tricks. By distracting the audience, they hide the sleight-of-hand that brings forth rabbits or cuts assistants in half. We expect illusion on the stage and are entertained by our inability to see beyond it. When illusion and make-believe are part of real life, however, our inability to spot the deception is no longer entertaining. It may be life threatening.

Some of us rely a lot on illusions and sleight-of-hand in our relationships, particularly the bad ones. By concentrating on the illusions, we miss the reality. This chapter helps you to spot the distracting illusion and see the reality. Recognizing what is really happening and what is make-believe offers a better understanding of the alternatives when you are faced with importance choices in a relationship.

In relationships, illusions are not magic tricks; they are lies. It may be a lie your lover tells you, or one you tell yourself to avoid acknowledging the hopelessness of your partner. When a person creates an illusion of being something he or she is not, he or she is, in essence, lying. Some people lie out of habit, the way addicts use drugs. Others lie to manipulate.

There are four common ways people get trapped in illusions:

- Self-deceivers who believe they can change or transform their lover
- Self-deceivers who mistake infatuation for love

- Outright liars, whether habitual or manipulative
- Abusers who profess care when actually they want control

CHANGING SOMEONE

People have to want to change. You can't control someone else's behavior. Sometimes tragedy, or an ultimatum, inspires a transformation, but only if the person involved wants to do it. Alcoholics Anonymous, for example, demands that the drinker—not relatives, friends, bosses, or coworkers—make the decision to stop drinking. The same is true in most drug treatment programs. And it is certainly true in therapy.

None of us can control any behavior but our own. You may decide to act differently in response to a lover's actions. You may insist on being treated more respectfully. But if a partner doesn't respond to your changes, your choices are to accept the reality of the relationship or learn what you have to do to leave.

Many movies idealize the process of changing behavior, leading us to believe it is easy. But movies are fiction, scripted by writers. Real life doesn't follow a script.

Remember, you can control only your own behavior. You cannot hold yourself responsible for what someone else does. For example, if you live with an abusive person, you can't make him or her stop being abusive. You can recommend therapy or give an ultimatum to stop the abuse or you will leave. Staying may encourage the behavior.

Leaving may not stop it, but it gets you out of danger. It requires, however, a degree of financial security and self-confidence often lacking in an abusive relationship. For those who feel trapped in a dead end, finding support and developing skills that lead to independence are important first steps. They can also provide the basis for an ultimatum that can shock a partner into a new level of respect and agreement.

Many people resist reality because that gives them a sense

of control and security. If you believe that you can change a lover by your actions, you don't feel as threatened. Recognizing that your empathy is usually counterproductive is scary, because you don't know what may happen next. This is particularly dangerous if the lover is abusive.

Women who are the victims of abusers often believe they are responsible for their partner's violence. If only they did things right, showed more sympathy and understanding, recognized their mate's problems, they wouldn't get hit. Making you feel guilty is part of the pattern of abuse. Nothing can prevent their reactions if they don't want to change. Pretending you can change them only makes you the target of more abuse. And if there are children, it not only makes them potential victims but also sets a pattern of behavior that will probably continue in their own families.

The illusion that you can change a mate's behavior is no more real than the hallucinations of drug users and psychotics. And no more useful. A promise to change that is not followed by action is worthless, no more believable than a drinker's promise to stop drinking—as soon as the bottle is empty.

INFATUATION VS. LOVE

Some of us have had a vacation fling, a brief affair, a teenage crush on the newest film star. And most of us recognized that the primary emotion driving the relationship was infatuation, not love. The lover moved on, or we did, knowing that love was still to come.

Some people, at particularly needy periods, get confused. They mistake the affection, companionship, and temporary excitement for the real thing. Because they so desperately want someone to care, to make a difference, to provide them with a sense of belonging, they convince themselves that temporary infatuation is love.

Kathy and Bruce

Kathy and Bruce were in their late thirties. He owned an appliance store, and she worked for a small company; both put in long hours. They came home to their three children and rarely argued. Their marriage had lost all passion and emotion.

When a consultant arrived to help with accounting at Kathy's office, she was very impressed with him. Barney was smart, good-looking, and friendly. After his striking presentations to the executive board, she suggested lunch. It was the first of many. The third lunch expanded into a quick visit to a nearby motel, and Kathy felt that she had never met anyone like Barney. She was in love, or so she thought.

Everything seemed right. He loved her. He was bright, interesting, successful, attractive, dynamic, and social. He had a great sense of humor and enjoyed talking to and being with her.

Kathy considered a divorce. When she discussed this with Barney, she finally learned he was already married—and didn't want to change wives. Over the next few months, Barney gradually became irresponsible and unreliable. He missed their dates and called off their trysts. It took her days to reach him on the phone.

He frustrated her enough to slow the relationship but not to end it. Once, he didn't call for a month. He always had a good excuse—his wife was suspicious, he had to spend time with his kids. Kathy began to hear about other women he had dated since his marriage. He was uninterested in her work or the MBA classes she was taking. When they were together he was full of laughs and games, but he refused to entertain serious discussions about anything, especially their relationship.

In time, Kathy realized that Barney didn't care for her beyond their noontime trysts. He never remembered her problems and grew bored if she discussed them. He had no interest in long-term planning beyond their next lunch date, based on his schedule, not hers. When she was upset, he pacified her with promises but never followed through. He refused to go beyond the quickie lunch and motel routine, not even a movie or dinner date. He wouldn't consider leaving his wife.

Kathy realized that she had fantasized her involvement with Barney and what they shared was infatuation, not love. She recognized that Barney had nothing to offer her. More importantly, she didn't trust him and knew he was dishonest. She couldn't believe much of what he said, and she had nothing in common with him apart from lunch and sex. She ended the affair and began marital counseling with her husband.

Before long, it was clear that as Kathy and Bruce pursued their separate careers, she had become very depressed by the lack of a relationship with her husband and the demands on her time that kept her from her children. Despondent and angry at Bruce for not appreciating her need to spend more time with the children, she embraced a new relationship to get back at him. In this instance, marital counseling sessions were effective in resolving her dissatisfactions and reconciling the relationship.

There are several distinctions between love and infatuation. Understanding them can provide some perspective, and honestly evaluating your own relationship may allay the perceived pain of ending it. As the story of Kathy and Bruce demonstrates, people are often susceptible to infatuation when they are depressed and/or angry at a partner:

- Love means strong feelings of care and concern for each other. This is why love is often described as a transcendent experience. Someone in love transcends his or her own needs to focus on the beloved, both in bed and out.

Infatuation is characterized by focusing on how wonderful the beloved makes you feel. For example, a partner who doesn't care about your orgasm is infatuated, not in love.

◆ Love energizes people and prompts them to be expansive in all aspects of their life. Infatuation shrinks people. It encourages them to focus on the relationship, restricting the outside world, much like a drug abuser likes to nestle with the source of the addiction.

◆ Lovers find that sex becomes more associated with shared affection and less with raw arousal. With infatuation, sex is best at first and tends to get kinkier with time to keep the excitement.

◆ Love progresses from an initial state of passion to one of attachment and, ultimately, commitment. The passion is replaced by deeper feelings of caring and trust. It resurfaces when coaxed, but usually the memory is enough. Infatuation also starts with passion, but when it dissipates what follows is withdrawal and disinterest.

◆ Love fosters long-range planning—house, children, career. Infatuation focuses on short-term goals—vacations, entertainment.

◆ Lovers can abstain from sex and tolerate absences the infatuated typically cannot.

◆ Lovers are preoccupied with the well-being of their beloved; the infatuated are more concerned with being abandoned.

◆ Love means growth and change. It implies aging together, uncaring of the designs the years add. The lover who wants to stay perpetually young may be more "in love with love" than loving.

If what you have is infatuation masquerading as love, that is enough reason to pack up and move on—unless that's what you are looking for. If it's real love, but still bad, then you may need some of the strategies and techniques discussed in later chapters to get yourself away. As already discussed, understanding why and how you are attached to someone who is bad for you is the first step to falling out of love . . . and landing on your feet.

The first part of this chapter discussed illusions we create for ourselves, but just as frequently someone else is actively changing reality for us. Some people knowingly lie to us. Others lie to themselves as well as to the people around them. If any of the following types of liars sound familiar, your best intentions probably can't save the relationship.

LIARS AND DAMNED LIARS

Although white lies may be the oil of civilization, someone who consistently distorts the truth suggests a serious problem. Some liars are manipulators; they use their stories to control others by limiting their access to knowledge. Then there are habitual liars, people who don't notice or care about truth or honesty. I discuss each type in detail because the fact of lying may not be as important as why the person lies. If you recognize the characteristics of your partner, it is another warning that your relationship is built on quicksand.

MANIPULATORS

These liars want to be in control. Knowledge is power, and by controlling the truth and who hears it, they are in command. They may fear commitment, for example. Men who are unwilling to commit to marriage tell lies to avoid the traps they see everywhere. The lies begin immediately, because they know they will not get dates if they admit that marriage is out of the question.

Jerry and Paula

Jerry tried marriage for five years. He loved his wife, but shortly after the ceremony he began to feel trapped. When she started talking about children, he nearly panicked. He lost all ambition, refused to think about the future, and became more and more irresponsible. His wife got fed up and divorced him. Jerry enjoyed the bachelor's life for twelve years. As soon as a girlfriend mentioned marriage, Jerry was out the door, and he never looked back.

At thirty-nine, Jerry was tall, muscular, and handsome, working as a systems analyst for the government. Paula was thirty-six and a teacher at Head Start when they met. She was in heaven. He seemed to want marriage as much as she, frequently asking for reassurance about her feelings. He wasn't at all reluctant to talk about the importance of their relationship.

Just before they officially announced their engagement, they went on vacation. That's when Paula first noticed that Jerry's behavior was changing. He complained about her nonstop talking and her frequent calls to him at work. He ridiculed her interest in buying a vacation house. He insisted that they save more money before getting engaged, saying there was no hurry.

Paula noticed other ominous signs. He was late for many of their dates. He talked about needing space and freedom. At first, she tried to ignore the portents, but she could not deny he was taking the freedom he demanded. When she could get him to talk about it, he blamed her for being too demanding and controlling but said he still loved her and wanted to marry her.

During one of their arguments, Jerry fled to the safety of another girlfriend. He was so frustrated with Paula's demands that he found himself proposing to Annie. Later, he broke the engagement to Annie and even briefly resumed his affair with

Paula. But she was wise to his manipulations. He disappeared whenever their relationship seemed to show signs of commitment and permanency. Paula decided to end her own misery and put Jerry out of her life for good.

For those with a fear of commitment, the early stages of a new relationship are very intense, with all the usual signs of falling in love. It is only when the new lover starts talking about living arrangements or even wedding plans that the manipulative liar kicks into fifth gear.

These people are threatened by the idea of forever. Marriage means confinement, and even living together involves restrictions. When the subject first arises, they may provoke arguments to slow things down. Manipulative liars may truly be in love and at first desperately want you. But they begin to lose interest when you ask for promises of longtime security.

Planning dates a week in advance puts pressure on manipulating liars. They prefer last-minute arrangements, arguing for spontaneity. They also avoid introducing you to friends or coworkers. Why should they? You won't be around long. They may have several other lovers and so are adept at lying to explain absences.

Often, manipulators choose others who cannot make commitments either. They may have affairs with someone who is married or going through a divorce. If given an ultimatum to change, manipulators end the relationship, then blame the ex-partner. They project their problems onto you, accusing you of being too intense, pressuring them to make decisions, demanding a decision they aren't ready to make.

HABITUAL LIARS

For some people, the truth is not an option. They tend to fall into four categories:

➤ Nonassertives

➤ High-energy types (discussed in greater detail in Chapter 5 as Mr. Excitement)

➤ Sociopaths (futile attractions, also described in Chapter 5)

➤ Addicts

For habitual liars, lying is an easy, effective, and convenient means to an end. They rarely feel any sense of guilt and convince themselves that the end result is in everyone's best interests. We all use social lies occasionally, but habitual liars go well beyond this. Their every excuse can be predicted and their every action foretold. This is the pattern of a lifetime. Every relationship ends the same way, because they do the same things.

NONASSERTIVES

These people lie because they are afraid to talk about real feelings. Often, they use evasion to avoid a painful or difficult situation. For example, a self-employed man may tell his wife someone failed to pay him rather than admit he lost the money gambling.

Gregg and Bonnie

Gregg hates to say no to anyone. He also likes approval and applause. When he and Bonnie married, he told her that he was the assistant manager at the small optical company where he worked. It was only a matter of time before he would get a raise and a promotion. At work, he actually had little responsibility, but his family thought he ran the company.

For years, he remained charming and upbeat. He told his coworkers what they wanted to hear and rarely refused a request. At home, he was equally easygoing. He never criticized or complained about his job. Everything was great: The raise was only a few months away; the promotion due any week. Unwilling to confront anything, Gregg always promised Bonnie to take care of any problems, then promptly forgot about them. Eventually Bonnie realized that the raise and promotion and Gregg's boastful tales of work were all lies.

Rationalizations open the door to lies. Gregg would tell Bonnie not to wait up for him because he had to work late. In reality, he was meeting his buddies at a favorite hangout. He knew that would upset her, so he lied to avoid the argument, explaining to himself that it was better than distressing her.

Using such rationalizations, nonassertive liars convince themselves that no one is hurt by their lies. Actually, when the lies are discovered, the victim is often furious and distrustful. When Bonnie discovered that Gregg had been lying to her for years, she was shocked. Once she faced the fact that he could not change, she got a divorce.

Because they have difficulty expressing their feelings, nonassertive liars have trouble saying no. Afraid of rejection or anger, they often lie to avoid hurting your feelings. If the truth might bring criticism or disappointment, nonassertive liars will ignore it. They are dependent on social approval, often bragging about their lack of enemies or the high regard others have for them.

For this type, anything that might bring anxiety or confrontation is best avoided by any means necessary. Because they lack a strong identity, they may appear to be hypocrites because they go along with any expressed opinion. By always trying to please those around them, even through lies, they can keep friendships going that might otherwise deteriorate.

Like Gregg, they keep to a superficial level on everything. Going deeper might bring up inconsistencies that could cause problems, so it is much easier to ignore them. As a result, nonassertive liars are seen as nice and typically have a lot of friends. Trusting mates find them very affectionate and selfless. It is only when the lies are uncovered that those actions have a more negative hue.

By justifying their lies as necessary to avoid hurting someone, they deny any evil intent. Even when they have fallen out of love, they prefer to have you make a decision and often go to great lengths to be irresponsible and frustrating. If confronted, they often deny any change in their feelings, refusing to acknowledge or even discuss the true situation. So strong is their need for approval that they rarely criticize anyone, preferring instead to remain everyone's buddy and admirer.

HIGH-ENERGY TYPES

This personality lies to speed up the action. Many high-energy people thrive on excitement, and revealing a truth such as "I'm overextended and shouldn't use my credit card" can slow things down. While not everyone with a high energy level is a habitual liar, many do gloss over details.

Peter and Mary

At forty-nine, Peter loved excitement. His preferred sport was skiing, but he would try almost anything. His fiancée, Mary, was fifteen years his junior. They took sport-oriented vacations together at Peter's suggestion. He had lots of friends and seemed to be financially settled. The courtship was wonderful, but when they began living together, Peter's stories began to fall apart.

Mary realized that Peter didn't really have a job with an exporting business. Instead, he spent his time at sports and with his friends. He didn't really do anything that earned money. He had a few odd jobs and hoped Mary would pick up his bills. Eventually, she recognized that he said whatever he thought she wanted to hear. He showed no signs of growing or even changing. Instead of looking for work, he visited his friends and flitted from surf to slope with the seasons. Mary decided she needed someone more responsible and less glib.

SOCIOPATHS

Unlike the previous liars, sociopaths don't really care about approval or being liked. They lie about everything all of the time because it doesn't make any difference to them.

Mario and Catherine

When Mario met Catherine, he told her he was in the trucking business. It was slow, but he expected it to turn around at any time. He was a college graduate who had a lot of important friends and saved his money. He had been the victim of a dishonest partner who stole his previous business, and what was left went to a vindictive ex-wife, but he had never had any problems with the law. Mario was exciting, confident, and charismatic, and he adored Catherine.

It wasn't until after they were married that Catherine discovered that Mario was really a criminal. He made money selling stolen goods, and his friends were all gangsters. His entire past was a fantasy. He had not gone to college; he had no former business or nasty divorce. He never considered honest work and thought those who did too stupid for words. When Catherine confronted him about his lies, he laughed and joked about them but didn't deny lying. Catherine decided that although Mario lied about everything, she was honestly getting a divorce.

Sociopaths have no guilt about lying because they don't care about the truth or someone else's regard for it. They cover one lie with another. These people get a thrill from lying and may admit to falsehoods just to watch your reaction. They also use lies to tease, to show disdain and lack of respect for everyone else.

Sociopaths often pass lie detector tests because they don't feel any guilt about lying. The tests are designed to pick up on the physical reactions most people show when questioned about falsehoods. But for the small minority who have no qualms about lying, a polygraph registers their lack of response as telling the truth.

ADDICTS

Like drug users, addictive liars minimize and deny the destructive potential of their lies. They enjoy lying, which gives them a high by delivering big results for a small effort. It also gives them a sense of power and control.

Ruth and Joe

Ruth couldn't stand stress or boredom. If she couldn't be distracted, she became anxious and suffered anxiety attacks. Joe was annoyed with her problems after fifteen years of marriage, and their relationship deteriorated. Her lack of self-esteem and self-confidence made working impossible. She had two children nine and fourteen, but when they were in school she was bored at home alone. Joe's criticism made her feel weak, inferior, stupid, childish, and helpless.

Overwhelmed by her negative feelings, she started using cocaine because, "It was the only thing I could control." She said it distracted her from her boredom and relieved her anxiety attacks. But to cover up her drug use, she began lying regularly. She lied to Joe and other family members. She lied to friends. She even lied to herself, promising, "I'll stop soon; I don't need the drugs; I won't let my use interfere with raising the children."

Instead, she became more and more dependent on cocaine and then on alcohol. As her need for money to pay for the drugs increased, so did the lies. Joe never knew when she was telling the truth and when she was lying. As her lies unraveled, Joe grew even more distant, and they finally separated.

Ruth was able to stop using the drugs after the pressures of a bad marriage eased, but lying had become a habit. Like other drug users who lie to hide their abuse, she found that a much more difficult habit to break.

Addictive liars use their falsehoods to ward off the stresses of life. If confronted about their lies, they often become angry and abusive. Like other addicts, they frequently promise to stop but relapse. Lying creates a distorted reality that is similar to the illusions created by drugs. Both involve escapism and fantasy. Both are crutches. By creating dependence, they erode self-esteem. Addictive liars suffer from fears of inadequacy and inferiority. Lying is a defense against these feelings that makes the addict feel less vulnerable and more in control.

ABUSERS: CARE VS. CONTROL

Abusers typically suffer from strong feelings of inadequacy, inferiority, and insecurity. They come on sweet to attract a relationship, but later, convinced no one could really love them, they rely on control to keep you around. They try to isolate you, eliminating any friends or even relatives who threaten their self-esteem, which is almost everyone. They become obsessed with control, dehumanizing you in an abusive cycle that may have begun with real care and concern.

Recognizing the difference between an abuser and a truly caring partner is difficult.

Sophia and Alberto

When Sophia met Alberto she was very impressed with his concern for her welfare. He seemed more caring and sensitive to her needs than any of the other men she had dated. When she was with him, she felt totally safe and protected. He seemed to anticipate her needs and look for ways to protect her. Alberto was loving and considerate, and they developed what seemed to be a wonderful relationship.

Sophia's father was the captain of the local police force and her mother taught at the local grammar school. Sophia grew up with a middle-class lifestyle that emphasized safety and protection. She had friends watching over her, and saw it as a sign of love.

Once, Sophia was driving in a neighboring town when her car broke down. Parked on the side of the road, she got out and flagged a police car. The officer called her father's station and reported her situation. Within a few minutes, Sophia's car was surrounded by flashing lights and friendly cops. She was driven home and her car taken for repairs.

Alberto's early attentiveness seemed very similar to the concern Sophia was used to, and she fell in love quickly. Alberto paid attention to her needs and spent all of his free time with her. She did think it odd that he didn't seem to have any friends of his own because she thought he was the most lovable of men. When she went off with her friends or visited her parents, Alberto always called to make sure she was okay. If she went elsewhere, he asked her to call him to let him know where she was.

The first sign of a problem after they married came the day Sophia went to the mall with friends and forgot to tell Alberto where she was and when she would return. When she came back, Alberto was furious. Sophia was shocked by his anger, but she dismissed the incident at first. In time, she realized that something was seriously wrong. He seemed to be obsessed with her, and she, in turn, became preoccupied with anticipating his outbursts.

When she tried to discuss this with him, he denied having a problem. It was her fault for not telling him what he wanted to know. Several of her friends suggested that she leave him. Sophia wasn't willing to give up on her marriage yet, but Alberto seemed to know she was growing more dissatisfied with him. He insisted he couldn't live without her and defended his obsessive behavior as evidence of his total devotion.

He tried to tighten his control over her. He manipulated

her friends into fights with him, then refused to see them. He pressured Sophia to break off from them as well. When she balked, he verbally attacked her without relief until she agreed not to invite them to the house. She told Alberto she wouldn't see them at all but knew that was a promise she wouldn't keep. She already found it easier to go along with his demands than fight his jealousy.

Nevertheless, Alberto became increasingly insecure as he sensed Sophia moving away from him. He accused her of being unfaithful and insisted she not associate with any men. When he learned she had run into an old boyfriend, he found out where the man lived and confronted him. He warned the man to stay away from Sophia, and when the man denied any romance, explaining they met unexpectedly, Alberto attacked him.

Sophia found out about this and threatened to leave. Alberto's answer was to punch her. As she lay on the floor, he started to strangle her. Sophia thought she was going to die, but Alberto let her go with the admonition that she behave herself. He also made her promise that she would not tell her father what had happened. Sophia was terrified.

She tried therapy with the hope that somehow her marriage could be fixed. Alberto was not interested in changing, and he was bitterly opposed to her going and tried to force her to quit. Sophia became so fearful that she bought a pager to notify her father if anything happened to her. In the course of all of this, Sophia's self-esteem plummeted and she became depressed and anxious.

Once Alberto realized that Sophia was intent on seeing me in therapy, he decided to come to the sessions. It soon became obvious that he was interested only in trying to manipulate Sophia to stay with him. In the sessions, he readily admitted abusing Sophia but insisted he had changed. He professed great love for her, showering her with gifts and promises. He agreed with everything Sophia said and pleaded for another chance. Sophia relented but soon found the same pattern of constricting control and abuse emerging. This was paralleled by his subtle attempts to minimize and discredit what came out in therapy.

Abusers, both verbal and physical, appear to show intense care and concern for you at first. But the questions about time spent away from them are really the first steps toward control. Abusers monitor their mate's every move, wanting to know whom you see and where you go. Abusers are easily jealous, suspecting that everyone else is interested in you.

You typically feel safe and protected when you start dating a potential abuser because of the all-encompassing attention to everything you do. Abusers begin by anticipating your needs and trying to shield you from adversity. In the initial stage of the relationship, abusers organize their life around you, apparently obsessed with you.

If accused of being controlling, abusers blame you. They often alienate your friends so that you are more dependent. Refusing to answer their queries provokes more verbal or physical abuse, so you give in to their demands. You become more isolated from sources of help.

Because abusers feel inadequate and inferior, they assume that no one will love them for themselves, so they try to control you through intimidation and violence. You often become more dependent on the abuser even while growing more fearful, since potential support from friends and family have been eliminated. As a result, partners in abusive relationships often feel trapped.

By accusing you of being flirtatious, or cheap, or unfaithful, abusers justify, at least in their minds, the use of violence. Abusive people usually have a history of abuse in the family, so physical violence seems the appropriate response.

At the same time, abusers are often dependent on the victim and express that need at least verbally. That makes you feel wanted and instills a false sense of security—"He really needs me so I won't be abandoned." In fact, abusers rarely leave, but they may end up killing you.

After the abuse, especially if it is physical, the abuser is usually remorseful, offering flowers, presents, and promises of reform to regain your trust. Because drugs and alcohol are often involved, the remorse and promises to change rarely last longer than the next binge. Abusers have little interest in therapy. If they do agree to go along, they try to use it as another way of controlling you.

If you are involved with an abuser, it is best to seek therapy alone. Once you have regained your self-esteem and bearings, you may want to try marital sessions, but beware that the abuser may attempt to manipulate the therapist into pressuring you.

Victims of abusers are usually too humiliated or browbeaten to report the violence. Domestic abuse is one of the most underreported of crimes, especially in middle- and upper-class homes.

Living with a lie is always difficult, whether it is your illusion that your partner will change or the web of falsehoods about his or her work and position. Once you identify and understand this pattern in your own life, you can begin to make changes.

Lying is only one sign of serious trouble. The next chapter discusses another ominous signal—the triangle.

❧ 3

Love Triangles (Affairs)

TRIANGLES, LIKE LYING, ARE SERIOUS SIGNS. THEY ARE evidence that a relationship is no longer satisfying, that one or both partners have turned to an outsider to meet emotional or physical needs. Understanding the hidden meanings, manipulative ploys, and power plays in a third-party situation may reduce the resentment of a betrayed partner and provide for a less emotional decision about the future of the relationship.

Not all love triangles involve sex. And not every affair represents the end of an ongoing relationship. Most people recognize a sexual affair as a serious betrayal of trust, but the relationship between two people becomes seriously unbalanced when *any* outsider becomes privy to the secret feelings of either one.

Including a third person usually indicates a serious problem. The extra person is almost always a special friend of only half the pair and may not even know the other one. The outsider may be a lover, a close friend, a confidant, or even a therapist. Although affairs are given a false glamour in novels and films, they do not always mark the end of a relationship. Sometimes the adultery is a temporary aberration and the other partner accepts it as such. Other times, the reliance on a third party marks a critical change in one person's feelings.

There are many reasons why an outsider gains access to a private relationship: as a confidant to help end the relationship; to alleviate a sense of sadness or depression that won't go away; as a sign of anger or revenge; or in response to a situation that offers opportunity and convenience. Recognizing the pattern may help reduce the sense of personal betrayal. Knowing that your mate refuses to control himself or herself—it is a personality trait to be unfaithful—can help define the terms of your relationship. Or becoming aware of a disloyal mate's insecurity and anxiety may give you clues as to how to strengthen your relationship. The examples and analyses in this chapter can help you cut through the emotional response to a third party and clear the way for a decision based on what you can expect in the future.

CONFIDANTS

Many people turn to a confidant when a love relationship is troubled. The outside person offers perspective and objectivity, providing a sounding board for complaints, real or imagined. The confidant can validate those complaints, agreeing they are cause for separation. Or the third party may point out the weaknesses in the argument. The third party can be a professional counselor, a family member, a longtime friend, or a new lover.

One reason for enlisting the support of a confidant is the very human need to believe oneself morally right. Especially in the breakup of a primary relationship, most people don't want to see themselves as responsible. A confidant who offers soothing sympathy provides a counterpoint to angry friends and family pointing accusatory fingers.

Sometimes the third party provides an opportunity to try a new identity. For someone considering the end of a long-term relationship, a confidant offers new friends, a new look, new interests. The newcomer may be the cause or effect of testing new directions, but he or she represents a change in the routine of daily life and an escape from the expectations of friends and family.

A confidant is not always of the opposite sex. He or she has to be someone not associated with the partner and willing to discuss the other person's feelings. Men often rely on women because other men are usually unavailable, but women typically turn to one another. For many women involved in a deteriorating relationship, another man would just be a complicating factor, although some do use male confidants.

Another reason for bringing in a third party is the problem of talking over changing feelings with family and friends. They are often unsympathetic with a revisionist view of a relationship's history. The outsider carries no historical baggage.

Playing the role of confidant has a great many risks. Typically, the outsider hears only one side and is strongly biased toward that partner. If the ultimate decision is to stay with the old partner, the confidant is often left behind. Typically, the only bond was the goal to end the relationship. When that goal changes, so does the confidant's role. If the other partner discovers the confidant's position, a great deal of anger generated by the disloyal mate is directed toward the outsider, making a continuing relationship impossible.

Ted/Carol/Alice

Ted is forty, an electronics specialist who works for his stepfather's large company. A quiet, easy-to-get-along-with type, he is accommodating and cooperative. He leaves household and family decisions to Carol, forty-two, who is somewhat aggressive and controlling.

Things began to change when Ted hired Alice, twenty-eight, to manage the company's books. Assertive, confident, and attractive, she developed a close relationship with Ted during the next two years. He told her about his family problems, and she encouraged him to take charge of his life. During their daily conversations, she sympathized with his complaints. When he told her he was unhappy in his marriage, Alice encouraged him to leave.

Ted told his wife he wanted a divorce. Carol was shocked. She had no idea that Ted was so unhappy. She insisted on marital therapy, and Ted reluctantly agreed. Ted's family supported Carol's conclusion that Alice was to blame. She was fired. Carol agreed to make changes to accommodate

Ted's wishes and they remained together. Ted, in turn, acknowledged that telling his problems to Alice was a violation of Carol's privacy and agreed to work on trust and communication problems with his wife. But Carol is obsessed with her anger toward the "other woman." In Carol's mind, she and Ted were victims of Alice's machinations.

For many people, the betrayal of vows and loss of trust represented by the arrival of an outsider are burdens too heavy for a relationship to carry. The disloyalty of a partner is considered as serious a treachery as any possible infidelity. Whether love affairs or friendships, a third party adds a layer of dishonesty in a relationship that masks serious underlying problems. The fact that Ted never developed a sexual relationship with Alice did not mitigate Carol's anger toward the other woman, although the lack of intimacy was a significant factor in Carol's belief that Ted had been manipulated by Alice. It is important to recognize that reliance on a confidant suggests that there are basic problems of communication between partners and shouldn't be dismissed as solely the work of an evil interloper.

DEPRESSION

Some people have affairs because they are depressed, and being desirable makes them feel better. This is especially true of someone who feels trapped in a relationship with someone who does not truly care for him or her. The relationship may be long gone, but the commitments remain. An affair provides a convenient means of venting frustrations and gaining additional gratification.

Wendy

Wendy had grown apart from her husband, Peter, during the past six years. Peter spent most of his time managing the stationery store he owned. Wendy worked as an assistant manager for a small real estate company. She was ambitious, whereas Peter seemed to be content just getting by. They had three children, ranging in age from twelve to twenty. She felt trapped and depressed, describing Peter "as very plain vanilla."

Brent was Wendy's supervisor. Charismatic and ambitious, he loved to have a good time, dine at expensive restaurants, and go to the theater and sporting events. Brent was a boost that made her able to withstand the week. She started having lunch with him and soon moved on to motel trysts.

After eight months of seeing Brent, Wendy began to feel the strain and tension from living two lives. She lied to Peter about her whereabouts and she lied to Brent when she downplayed her feelings for Peter. She realized that she would never leave Peter because she did not trust Brent. She even lied to herself about her true feelings—in fact, she enjoyed the romance and attention he gave her.

On a number of occasions, Wendy tried to break off the affair. Each time, she felt a strong emotional reaction, which led her back to Brent. Her friends encouraged her to leave Brent and go to counseling with Peter. She refused and gradually broke off contact with her friends.

Her world became progressively more constricted around Peter and Brent. She vacillated endlessly about what she should do. She bemoaned the deterioration of her character. She hated the constant stress and tension. In time, Wendy found that she reversed her thinking so much she had difficulty taking herself seriously.

One day, Brent announced that he was looking into a job in a nearby state. If he took the job, it would be impossible for their affair to continue. Brent seemed not to care especially and matter-of-factly discussed the potential of the new job.

Wendy was horrified. She realized that Brent didn't care about her. Even though the new job fell through, she decided to end the affair. It took six months of dwindling contacts before Wendy finally broke it off for good. When she attempted to repair her relationship with Peter, she realized it would not be easy. She had told Peter so many lies that she wasn't sure she knew how to be truthful anymore. She had lost trust in her own judgment and self-worth as well as in relationships. She also recognized how dependent she had become on the gratification she experienced from the affair.

Therapy helped Wendy recognize that she had used the affair to treat her depression. She also understood the damaging effects the affair had on her character.

Sometimes the potential for infidelity is overwhelming. Depressed people communicate neediness, and rescuers are attuned to these signals. The rescuer shows interest and empathy, two irresistible lures to someone wrapped in his or her own misery. Opportunity and convenience—the hidden supports for most affairs—ensure that something will happen.

Starting an affair energizes people. For someone who has been depressed, unable to concentrate at work, and easily distracted at home, the initial surge of pleasure is empowering. Suddenly all things are possible and doable. The need to see the lover requires planning, schedules, and timetables, so work gets done and assignments are met.

There are valid chemical reasons why a love affair can alleviate depression, at least briefly. A "love chemical" (phenylethylamine or PEA) is released. A powerful stimulant, it is partly responsible for the passion people report in the early stages of a relationship. For a while it counteracts the effects of the depression, but like cocaine and other stimulants, its action is short-term.

When triggered for more than a few months, the effect wears down, creating the need for more stimulation. With drugs, the user takes more to maintain the effect. In a good relationship, a psychological state of peace and attachment fills the spaces left by reduced passion and the brain releases a new set of chemicals, called endorphins, associated with relaxation and comfort.

The initial rush of excitement and risk overwhelms the depressive at first. Anything seems worth that feeling. The person believes the affair can be kept in control and won't disrupt the rest of life. A dual mentality develops: One side sees work, delay of pleasure, and long-term commitment as the best way to assume responsibilities; the other side recognizes the ease and efficiency of obtaining enjoyment from the affair.

It is similar to the choice an addict faces: to obtain quick satisfaction from drugs or longer-term pleasure from the complexity of hard work and interaction with family and friends. And like the addict, a person having an affair knows there will be withdrawal if it ends. Keeping the affair going provides both an antidepressant and a stimulating pleasure, powerful incentives for maintaining it.

ANGER OR REVENGE

Many people, particularly women, attribute their decision to have an affair to a need for revenge or as an outgrowth of anger at their spouse. The anger is typically sparked by the feeling that the relationship is essentially unfair. The man is seen as either abusive, neglectful, unconcerned, or uncaring. The woman feels that there is no relationship and either seeks one to fulfill her needs or to get back at the partner.

Linda and Jerry

Linda knew Jerry had a drinking problem before they married, but she hoped her love and presence would help him give it up. After four years, nothing had changed. Every night, Jerry sat in front of the television, channel surfing for sports shows and guzzling rum and Coke. He had no ambition and showed interest in nothing except the drinks and television.

When they went out, Linda was a nervous wreck because Jerry always created a scene. It didn't matter if they were with friends or relatives, or whether the discussion was about politics, sports, or the weather; Jerry would find a way to get into an argument with someone. Linda resented his selfishness and lack of concern for her feelings and embarrassment.

One night, she had planned a big evening with friends—a Broadway show and an elegant dinner afterward. As usual, Jerry had a couple of drinks before they left the house, making them late meeting the other couple. At the theater, he had several more Cokes, each time adding rum from the flask he had brought along. By the time the show ended, the flask was empty but Jerry wasn't.

At the restaurant, the drinking continued. When the entrees arrived, so did Jerry's argumentative side. He started a political discussion that rapidly degenerated into an argument, accusing the other man of being a bleeding-heart liberal who sided with communists. By the time the meal ended, conversation was at a standstill.

Back home, Linda confronted Jerry, but he insisted she should have supported his position. He refused to acknowledge that his behavior was the cause of the problem. Furious and depressed, and realizing he wasn't going to change, Linda moved out and began divorce proceedings. She also called an old friend of Jerry's and seduced the man over dinner. Linda knew that Jerry would find out eventually and hoped he learned of the affair before the divorce became final.

OPPORTUNITY

One of the main reasons that people stray is because the opportunity is there. This is especially true of men. Many men working in large companies are exposed to younger women who look up to them. This is a great temptation. If the job involves convenient time away from home or liaisons with a coworker, the likelihood of an affair increases dramatically.

Research has shown that as many as 70 percent of married people have affairs at some point in the marriage, with opportunity and convenience the most commonly cited explanations.

If a spouse is unavailable—hospitalized, away on a long trip, engrossed in a major project, having a child, under a lot of stress—the partner may take advantage of an opportunity for infidelity. Or the disloyal partner may be seduced by someone who mistakes friendliness for real interest.

Roland

Roland insists that he loves his wife and that they have a great relationship. They regularly go out to eat, they socialize with friends, they share the household chores and the care of their daughter. Nevertheless, he has had many short affairs. He meets a lot of women in his business, and sometimes he has a brief affair with one of them. He is not interested in leaving his wife, nor does he feel there is a problem with his behavior. He claims that these other women are just for fun and games.

Whatever the reason for the affair, eventually unfaithful partners recognize that life is out of control. At this point, they become more impulsive and begin acting out. For example, they may make increasingly far-fetched excuses for not being home, developing a reputation for irresponsibility.

Pressuring someone to be responsible usually has the opposite effect. Rather than face the accusations of friends and family, a person having an affair often avoids them, spending time instead with the lover. He or she sinks into a private world, like the alcoholic who just wants to be with his drinking buddy or the workaholic who stays at the office.

Like other addictions, an affair has long-range effects, often not immediately apparent. The dishonesty necessary for infidelity develops thinking and behavior patterns that endure long after the affair is over.

Another hidden result of an adulterous affair is the debilitating effect it has on a person's character. Gratification is easy and convenient. Even if the affair ends, the lesson has been learned and may very well transfer to other activities. The spouse who has had an affair may shun gratification from traditional sources and avoid the necessary time and effort in favor of easier approaches. As such, an affair can have a long-lasting effect on personality and one's approach to life's tasks.

Even though most people recognize the problems the affair is causing, they become less and less able to control them. The affair provides emotional satisfaction that is more powerful than the intellectual consideration of what is best. In this manner, they learn to distrust thinking and accept acting on impulses, another dangerous lesson.

The affair introduces the need to lie—usually to both the spouse and the lover—which further erodes a personality. Often the lover becomes an object used to obtain gratification. The denigration of the lover from person to object sets another disastrous pattern—using people for a selfish benefit without consideration of their needs.

The maneuvers required to maintain an adulterous affair drain energy and limit productivity. More and more time is spent with the lover at the expense of all other aspects of life. Work, friends, family suffer. Financial problems arise and soon the spouse and children start acting out.

Unfaithful partners become more isolated. Usually they refuse to consider the consequences of their action because deep down they know they are being irresponsible and self-absorbed. They may restrict their lives to their lovers and the bare requirements of work and family. Since most of the people in their life don't sympathize, they become solitary and distrustful of others. Many people in this position develop physical symptoms from the stress—anxiety attacks, headaches, gastrointestinal disturbances, sleep problems.

This situation can continue until a crisis occurs. The

spouse may deliver an ultimatum. The lover gets tired of being the "other." Sometimes children spark the crisis, acting out from the tensions in the family.

Even if the immediate crisis is resolved and the affair ends, the underlying problems remain. The causes of the affair must be explored and the holes in the marriage discussed and worked on. In some cases, a new, stronger relationship develops.

Just as often, the underlying problems are too widespread to save the relationship. The marriage is not fulfilling the needs of one or both partners. Then both people develop a new life. Adulterous partners may also have to heal the wounds to self-esteem that develop from losing control over their lives. They have to unlearn the dangerous habits—treating people as objects, lying, allowing emotional impulses to control actions—that are a part of an illicit affair.

Ending an affair does not necessarily end the love or infatuation. That can demand the same degree of concentration and understanding as concluding any relationship. Confusing infatuation with love or being in love with an impossible partner presents the same kind of obstacles and requires the same process of breaking free.

Everyone involved in a triangle is a victim. They all become actors in a drama no one is directing, controlled by the impulses of those around them. Even children are affected. The lack of honesty and trust between parents creates an inherently abusive environment, one that does not provide any safety or security. Children see one or both parents out of control, acting on selfish impulse and without regard for consequences—poor role models for developing personalities.

The betrayed spouse must confront the dishonesty of the past and the distrust of the future. He or she also faces the havoc created within the family by the introduction of a third person. Other problems include the disrespect shown by the unfaithful partner and the loss of self-esteem and self-confidence of the one who has been betrayed.

The person who initiated the affair also has to face up to the situation, including whatever prompted the infidelity. There are also the newly learned negative personality changes discussed earlier—lying, impulsive behavior, objectifying people, instant gratification.

Finally, the lover loses. Even if the affair breaks up a marriage, the lover is usually left behind, a reminder of a difficult time. If the affair turns into marriage, the lover worries about the spouse's commitment to vows. After all, no one knows better than a lover who becomes a spouse how unimportant those vows were in the previous marriage.

Triangles, whether sexual or not, mean dishonesty, distrust, and disloyalty. The betrayed partner must decide whether to continue as a couple or end the relationship. If the decision is to pull out, the next few chapters can help lessen the pain, guilt, and dependence.

❧ 4

Rogue Lovers

Some people just don't make good partners. They have behavioral or psychological problems that prohibit trust, inhibit empathy, and destroy love. At the same time, they are often charming, energetic, affectionate, and attractive. Or they are so needy as to rouse pity and concern. People involved with them are often indecisive about ending the relationship because there seem to be so many uncertainties.

For those involved with the types I call rogue lovers and futile attractions, often just understanding the predictable—if negative—behavior is enough to bring a decision. Recognizing that some of the best and worst traits of your lover are characteristics of difficult personality types, not unique quirks, can be eye-opening. Many women, for example, stay with impossible men out of a sense of loyalty that they perceive as love. But when they recognize that their partner is not showing any loyalty in return, their lingering emotional attachment is usually broken.

Rogue lovers frustrate and anger their partners. Often their behavior is the result of being indulged and humored because everyone finds that easier than fighting or putting up with the tantrums. Few of these types change on their own. Faced with an ultimatum and the loss of people important to them, they may be willing to try therapy.

Rogue types are not always easy to pick out. The extent of their problems may not be obvious until some time has passed. For people married to rogues, it is the building frustration and resentment that brings about a break, not necessarily a specific action.

In rogues, the negative traits are always present, but they

are intensified by any crisis or anxiety, real or imagined. Just being loyal and supportive is not enough to change their behavior; they need professional help.

Staying with these types out of loyalty can challenge even a strong person's self-esteem and identity. A rogue's partner is inevitably forced to follow a one-person agenda that takes no notice of anyone else's needs. For those in relationships with rogue lovers, it is often helpful to understand how rigid and calculating they are.

Frequently new patients begin outlining the problems in their relationship and I give them an exact description of their mate's actions or attitudes. They are usually surprised to discover how predictable some flamboyant personality types can be. The need for help or escape becomes clear when the pattern becomes so calculated.

With that in mind, what follows are personality types of rogue lovers—people too caught up in their own emotional problems to sustain an adult relationship. Their needs dictate the pace of the relationship, its degree of intimacy and responsiveness. In some types, the control extends to every aspect of life. It is the rogue who governs the relationship emotionally, financially, physically, socially, and psychologically.

VICTIMS

These people chronically blame others for anything and everything that happens in their lives. They are never at fault; it is always someone else who has done something to make their life impossible.

Shirley and Alex

Shirley suffered from heart disease and various minor ills. She blamed her foster parents for her illness, saying they had not cared for her and delayed medical treatment. She had come down with rheumatic fever, which left scarring on her heart valves. According to her, no one, including her doctors, appreciated how difficult her life was. She was also moody, negative, and pessimistic, and she blamed her husband for her irritability. Because he had good health and an easygoing disposition, Alex overlooked problems and didn't understand how hard things were for her. Shirley believed that even her children had turned against her, attracted by Alex's more endearing qualities.

When they first started going out, Alex was attracted to Shirley's beauty, and he derived a great deal of gratification from pleasing her. He sympathized with her moods and her complaints about friends and family members who were making her unhappy. Alex accepted her judgment that her foster parents were selfish and her friends jealous and spiteful. He assumed that her anger was justified and that once they got married she would be much happier.

The problems developed slowly. Since Shirley had suffered so much, she refused to work and demanded a housekeeper. At first Alex refused, but she continued to badger him, insisting that his stubbornness was making her heart condition worse, and he finally agreed. Their relationship improved—briefly—but his capitulation validated her feeling of being a victim and she became even more difficult.

When Alex developed prostate cancer, Shirley complained to friends and family, "Now look what I have to put up with!" Alex began to see that other people were not always responsible for Shirley's unhappiness. As is typical of the victim personality, Shirley found many other ways to blame Alex for her problems. He considered divorce, but for the sake of the children learned to adapt to her demands.

Rita and Roger

When Rita met Roger, she bitterly complained about her difficult childhood, how her parents, especially her father, controlled her. She enlisted Roger's support against her parents. Having a common enemy acted to forge a strong bond between them. She viewed Roger as the hero, someone who not only saved her but also was cast as a special, saintlike person. Roger had never experienced such love and adoration, and they married within a year.

Roger was amazed to find himself the villain several years later. Whenever they disagreed, Rita immediately assumed that he was taking advantage of her and she was the victim. Any attempt on his part to move her from that position proved futile. Rita's insistence on her victimization drove Roger away. The relationship deteriorated, becoming a self-fulfilling prophecy, and they eventually separated.

Shirley and Rita showed all of the traits of victims:

- They are externalizers, people who blame others for everything that happens.

- They are inclined to have depressive tendencies and be very moody.

- They have difficulty seeing anyone's point of view but their own.

- They choose as mates internalizers, people who take the blame for everything that happens, even if it is unwarranted: "I know he hit me from behind, but I should have checked my rearview mirror."

There is not much formal research on people who view themselves as victims. One way of determining whether your lover is a victim is to look for the other characteristics of depression, such as negativity, pessimism, low mental energy, cynicism, and irritability. If your lover is known for these traits among family and coworkers, you may want to reconsider your relationship—especially if everyone else disregards your mate's complaints and rationalizations.

Victims rarely respond well to a mate who tries to cure them. It takes an objective observer to help a victim understand and change the destructive pattern.

JEALOUS PARTNERS

For many people, jealousy is not a problem early in a relationship. They are flattered that their new partner is showing so much concern and interest. Once the jealous partner is sure of being loved and feels reassured, they reason, the jealousy will ease. But with extreme types, the deep-seated feelings of insecurity and inferiority create a jealous need constantly to control a mate.

It is a trait more often found in men than women, apparently as part of a primitive individual survival strategy. Every creature wants to promote not just its species but also its own uniqueness, that is, have children. A woman is assured that a child is hers; it comes out of her body. But a man can never be sure. He may be spending his time and energy providing shelter and food for another man's child, rather than passing on his own genetic heritage.

As a result, men are primarily aroused to jealousy by the fear of sexual infidelity, whereas women most often become jealous when confronted with emotional infidelity, the possibility that her mate might abandon her and her child for another woman.

Mark and Perri

Perri met Mark shortly after her divorce. She was extremely attractive, bright, and pleasant. Mark was intelligent but had trouble holding a job; he worked as a baggage handler at the airport. He spent a lot of time by himself, watching TV and gardening. He always seemed somewhat depressed and aloof and had no idea what Perri saw in him. He admitted in therapy that he thought that Perri was on a much higher plane and had no idea why she cared for him. He recognized that he would be more comfortable with someone on his level, but he could not let her go. At first, Perri enjoyed the security of their relationship and Mark's simple, straightforward approach to life. But his insecurity made him jealous.

In time, Perri grew to hate Mark's obsession. When he was with her he felt inferior, which made him uncomfortable, but when she was away he was overwhelmed with the fear that she would meet someone else. He continually questioned her on her whereabouts, tracking and monitoring everything she did. He called her several times a day at work. Mark doubted her explanations and checked with her friends. He hated going out with them and eventually alienated most of them.

When they were together, he suffocated her with his anxieties. He refused at first to go to therapy and reduced their life to an endless examination of her fidelity. When she insisted on therapy, he became apprehensive and tried to pressure her into stopping the sessions. He told her they couldn't afford them, and he didn't believe in therapy anyway. He even promised to change. He did make some token improvements, restraining his questions when she went out without him, but the changes were short-lived. Finally, she fulfilled his worst fears and left him. His fears and insecurities put an intolerable burden on the relationship.

Mark is a typical jealous rogue. We all feel jealousy at some time, and it can range from mild to severe. But when the following traits are persistent and extreme, the relationship lacks trust, and the condition is critical:

◆ Jealous rogues are insecure, anxious, and fearful of rejection.

◆ No amount of reassurance can quell their fears. This becomes a rationale to demand complete control of you, the only way they can feel assured and relieve their anxiety.

- They won't discuss their insecurity and need for reassurance, but instead focus on your behavior: Why were you late? Who were you talking to?

- Afraid of other influences and possible attractions, they try to isolate you from friends and family.

- Constant accusations and blame become self-fulfilling prophecies, driving you away and confirming their worst fears.

LONERS

In contrast to those rogues who fear commitment, loners shun relationships out of fear of rejection. They want a relationship but are too afraid of being abandoned to take a chance. They flee at the slightest hint of criticism, convinced they are avoiding total humiliation. There seem to be slightly more male loners than female. Typically, they have a friend or two who accept them unconditionally.

Alice and Geoffrey

Alice was in her late twenties when she met Geoffrey through a mutual friend. A grade school teacher with many friends, she was close to her parents and older brother and sister. She and Geoffrey began dating and were married barely a year later. Alice was attracted by his vulnerability, and she felt especially secure by his fearfulness of others. She felt that he would never leave her, which quelled her own insecurities and compensated her for his inadequacies.

Extremely bright, Geoffrey held strong leftist political views and didn't like to discuss them, fearing people would reject him if they knew his beliefs; only Alice was privy to his thoughts. He worked as a computer programmer for a defense contractor and worried that his politics could affect his job security.

Geoffrey made no effort to establish a relationship with Alice's family, although he didn't provoke any disagreements. When they visited Alice's parents, he often watched TV by himself. When the family visited Alice, he usually retired to another room. His reclusiveness caused bad feelings, and Alice's relatives openly mocked his politics and rudeness.

After the first few years of marriage, Alice gradually became distressed by her isolation. Geoffrey never wanted to go out. She loved people and had a strong need to be with her family and friends. Since her marriage, her contacts with them had nearly evaporated. Alice was always apologizing for Geoffrey's absence or disappearance, and her friends began avoiding her.

Alice worried about having a baby with him and suggested they not have children. Whenever Alice nagged Geoffrey enough to go out, he provoked an argument that ruined the evening. On her birthday, he fought with the waiter at the restaurant.

Finally Alice couldn't stand their reclusive life anymore. She reestablished ties with her family and friends and began living two lives, one at home with Geoffrey and one away with everyone else. For a while longer they kept the marriage going, but eventually they got a divorce.

The way Alice and Geoffrey met is typical of loners. Since they don't seek anyone out, a third party usually arranges an introduction. Many women find loners attractive at first since they are always home. Their fidelity is assured. Less attractive is their need for constant reassurance and their refusal to be around people. How do you know if your mate is a true loner or just dislikes your family?

♦ Loners have no tolerance for criticism or disapproval, requests for change, or disagreements. The normal everyday spat is enough to frighten them away.

➤ These rogues have low self-esteem and fear rejection and abandonment. Friends and acquaintances sense their longing for a relationship and view their fears as a challenge that can be overcome by the right person.

➤ They find excuses to avoid any social engagement and insist that you stay with them.

➤ Their fear of and disinterest in other people are the pattern of a lifetime. They have few friends and little contact with family.

Loners attract sympathy; that's why family and friends are always trying to fix them up. But loners' partners get frustrated. Their refusal to join in normal social activities builds anger and resentment. Humans are social animals and need contact with others of their kind. Loners are usually reluctant to seek treatment because it suggests change. They are very cautious about leaving the protective cocoon they have built. If you are in a relationship with a loner, and he or she will agree to therapy, you might have a chance.

DEPENDENT PERSONALITIES: MOLES

These rogues undermine relationships with their inordinate need to please. Dominating personalities are attracted to moles because they are so easygoing and agreeable. But moles are so anxious to accommodate their mates that they lose the respect of everyone around, including themselves.

Moles rarely show anger or express criticism. Gradually, their partners become frustrated and act more and more outrageously, hoping to provoke a reaction. A man married to a mole might, for example, openly admit an affair and insist on spending time with his mistress. In many cases, the wife accepts his demands, hoping her niceness will convince him to return. Usually it just provokes him further.

Many women say they have little interest in overly nice guys, complaining that they are weak, dull, boring, and lacking in confidence. Other women say that these rogues make them feel plain and unappealing. Women often look to relationships for excitement, stimulation, challenge, and productivity. Those women don't even notice moles.

Overly nice people may be worth pursuing. Or they may be masking their insecurity and inferiorities with accommodating behavior designed to lower your guard and make them attractive. Moles are very anxious, fearful of their self-worth, and lacking in confidence in their own opinions. They don't express their needs, so they are rarely met, which leads moles to stockpile resentments. They lack ambition and have difficulty with achievement. They can make you feel guilty if you try to break away. Life with moles is typically filled with the frustrations that accompany a lack of growth. Their fears prevent them from taking any risks or attempting any significant accomplishment.

Carol and Paul

Carol met Paul while shopping at a local market. He offered to help carry her packages. Although they were very different, they began dating. Carol was ambitious, intent on law school and a large family. Paul never spoke of his goals. He was content to be an assistant manager at a large company.

After their marriage, Carol would come home to find him watching TV. He never opened a conversation, suggested an outing, or proposed an activity. She began to spend more and more time on the phone with friends. She encouraged Paul to be more assertive and social, but he preferred to stay home, seeing his own friends only occasionally. As Carol pursued her goal, she gradually eclipsed Paul. They had very little in common and she barely noticed his presence.

Ultimately, she decided on a divorce because she could not imagine having children with him. She resented his lack of ambition and energy. She also resented his effect on her personality. She was very mean and nasty toward him and found herself becoming more impatient with others as well. For Carol, her marriage had become so lonely and empty she described Paul as more like a brother or roommate than a husband.

Mike and May

When Mike met May, she seemed perfect. She loved to make him happy and she was superaccommodating. Soon after they were married, Mike became disillusioned. May wasn't merely accommodating, she never expressed an opinion about anything. He complained that after a while being with May was like being alone. She offered him no feedback, leaving him to make decisions in a blind. She went along with anything he suggested, which he found distorted his personality. His strong political views became more insistent and rigid. Since May provided no opposition, when he discussed his views with others, he had difficulty with their refusal to accept his opinions.

His dominant traits became exaggerated, and they detracted from his relationships with friends and colleagues. He'd always been spontaneous, but May's encouragement led him to become irresponsible in the eyes of others. He canceled plans at the last moment with feeble excuses that worked only with May. His friends refused to tolerate his faults, and Mike became more dependent on May. When he complained about her dependence on him, he found no sympathy.

Mike also discovered that despite her agreeableness, May secretly resented him. She thought he was taking advantage of her. He acknowledged that he had become self-centered but attributed it to "living alone." Mike felt that May had more control over him than he had over her, although superficially it may have seemed the other way around. The reason, he said, was that "she forced me to assume all the responsibility; she refused to think. I don't know who she is, and I'm tired of feeling guilty for everything."

May complained at times about how Mike treated her, but not in a clear, straightforward fashion. For example, she griped about having to ask him for money whenever she wanted something but refused to deal with the checkbook. Then she insisted there was nothing she could do to change things. In this way, she also got back at Mike.

Concerned that his life revolved around May, Mike developed a relationship with another woman, one who was more independent and assertive. He saw her regularly but continued to live with May.

Moles, whether male or female, show similar characteristics:

- They are very passive, allowing you to make the major decisions in life, such as where you live, their work, friends, and social activities.

- They don't know how to express anger. As a result they are terrified that if they show their feelings, they will be unbearable.

- They have difficulty focusing on themselves, preferring to talk only about you.

- They have strong feelings of inadequacy, inferiority, and insecurity.

PASSIVE-AGGRESSIVES: SABOTEURS

These rogues also avoid confrontation, but they show their anger in devious ways. A saboteur's partner has no hint of a problem until, like the *Titanic,* he or she comes across the underwater obstacle. They always have a seemingly innocuous excuse—"I forgot" or "I got busy"—and they are very apologetic for their lapses.

Lily and Herb

Lily, an aggressive, dominant woman, had trouble finding a man who liked her. After numerous failed relationships, she started dating Herb, who seemed to have no trouble with her style. He was supremely accommodating and insisted that he loved making her happy. Lily, having been burned before by accommodating types, consulted a therapist. After meeting with both of them for a couple of sessions, the therapist advised Lily that Herb had difficulty asserting himself but could easily change with therapy. Shortly after that, they married.

Lily noticed that Herb did become less accommodating, but by creating little obstacles. For example, he told Lily that he had to eat earlier in the evening because he needed more sleep. Lily often worked late and now had to hurry to prepare meals. Herb ate faster and talked less. As a result, the meal ended quickly and became more of a chore than a pleasure.

There were other changes. Herb avoided talking to Lily's mother when she stopped by. He refused to stand up to his ex-wife's demands that inconvenienced Lily. He even allowed his twelve-year-old daughter to decide how to spend their time together, regardless of Lily's plans.

The agreeableness that she had liked at first, Lily came to despise. The relationship was exaggerating her own dominant tendencies, and she was having difficulty when anyone else showed independence. She became fearful of becoming too dependent on Herb. Lily returned to therapy and recognized that Herb was a passive-aggressive personality. She decided she would be less frustrated without him and moved out.

Saboteurs like Herb make you wonder who is truly at fault. They often seem so nice that you feel guilty for being angry with them. But the little frustrations continue to mount. Saboteurs can be very compliant and nice, but they drive you crazy. When you confront them—"Why didn't you pick up my clothes from the cleaners as you promised?"—they apologize, saying they simply forgot or something prevented them from doing it. However, something always prevents them from keeping their word.

Saboteurs are so out of touch with their feelings it's almost as if they don't have any. When you get angry, they don't yell back or even acknowledge their own anger. They just keep subtly undermining everything you do.

A saboteur can break out of the pattern. If he or she feels enough trust and confidence in you to express negative feelings, the hidden hostility diminishes, lessening the need for sabotage. But that may take too long. You may no longer feel comfortable reading your partner's meaning. Usually it takes therapy to help a saboteur understand the denial and buried emotions.

When Lily asked Herb if he wanted to go on a vacation, he said he had to work especially hard for a while. She had no idea if that was the truth or his way of refusing something she wanted. This confusion often destroys a relationship. The goal is to develop enough trust to allow the passive-aggressive to deal openly with feelings before they stockpile to dangerous levels. In the less severe cases this is often possible.

MOOD SWINGERS

Just as everyone sometimes experiences jealousy or self-pity, the occasional mood swing is a part of life. Someone doing well at work and involved in a loving relationship is going to feel happy. If that job disappears or a loved one becomes ill, that same person feels some anxiety, grief, sadness, uncertainty, and general irritability. But those are the expected responses to specific situations.

In mood swingers, the responses are unpredictable, the switches are rapid and without apparent cause, and the swings from energy and excitement to dissatisfaction and depression are frequent and intimidating. When one person's mood controls the household's actions, the situation is serious enough for outside intervention.

Richard and Liz

Richard met Liz at the large advertising agency where they both worked. Richard was a quiet, shy, introverted guy who loved to read and relax. He was not particularly ambitious or competitive. He seemed comfortable with himself and put little pressure on others. Liz, on the other hand, was extremely bright and articulate. She had received several honors in school and she did equally well at work. She enjoyed spending time with Richard and, after a one-year courtship, they got married.

The first year of their marriage was marred by unpredictable setbacks. Richard did not get the promotion he had expected. Liz's mother became ill and had to move in with them, so Liz cut back on her work to help care for her mother. Richard seemed to accept the situation and rarely complained.

During the next year, Liz insisted that Richard was uncharacteristically irritable and temperamental. In therapy, she blamed it on his lack of assertiveness, his difficulty communicating, his lack of caring, and on and on. Richard did not know what to make of her complaints. He felt she was either blowing things out of proportion or imagining them altogether. He tried to please her, but that didn't seem possible. When he listened to her point of view, she attacked him for not asserting himself. When he countered with his opinion, she accused him of not listening to her point of view.

Liz's moodiness erupted more and more frequently. At times, she went out of her way to please him. She was gracious and understanding, asking him what he wanted for dinner and preparing exactly what he asked for. Then, something minor would set her off. For example, if he came home fifteen minutes later than usual, she tore into him. She accused him of being inconsiderate and not caring about her.

Richard began to treat Liz as if he were walking through a minefield. He monitored her moods and tried to read her before he initiated any discussions. He was tense whenever she was around, wondering if it was all his fault. He never had similar problems with anyone else in his life.

Her moods were unpredictable. At times, if Richard backed off when Liz became angry and didn't contest her, she eventually settled down. But this approach did not always work. Richard had no idea when or why it did or didn't work. He also noticed that very little got by her.

He described her in therapy as "very aggressive. She has to respond to everything. She can't let anything go. If I come home late, if I wake up early and disturb her, if I forget to call, if I'm not aggressive at work, she can go into a rage and storm out of the house or wherever we happen to be, even a restaurant, and leave me there after unloading a tirade that can be extremely embarrassing. One time, I parked too far from the theater when it was raining and she accused me of doing it deliberately and she began to yell at me. She made such a commotion that I ended up driving home without her."

Liz often overcompensated for her outbursts the next day by being loving and attentive, not only with Richard but also with whoever had been the victim of a tantrum.

Richard was worried that he was becoming too dependent on Liz. She seemed to set up situations to manipulate his dependence on her. Liz insisted on pleasing Richard sexually, but that made him feel manipulated, not satisfied. He began to doubt her sincerity and feared being trapped by her. When she humiliated him in front of his parents, throwing a tantrum about his late working hours, it was the last straw.

* * *

The only thing predictable about mood swingers is how unpredictable their moods are. They can flip from one mood to another without warning. They may be up for a few days, then shift to a depressed, irritable mood. When they are up, they are loving and friendly. They often use this time to repair the feelings they created when they were down. The rest of the time, they overreact to minor offenses and have little tolerance for frustration.

Mood swingers are great at manipulating others, who can never be sure what will trigger a mood change. The subtle threat is usually enough to get them what they want.

CONTROLLERS

Control, or power, is a basic need. Most animals exhibit territorialism, mating battles, or some other kind of dominant-submissive behavior. In humans, this need takes a variety of forms. For some people, it is enough to live harmoniously and take responsibility for oneself. For others, proof of power comes from material success, recognition, or outright dominance. Still others, fortunately a minority, demand subservience often achieved through intimidation and/or violence. When one person's need for power interferes with anyone else's control of his or her life, the potential for abuse increases.

Controlling perfectionists and bullies are the types most likely to restrict your freedom. It is difficult, if not impossible, to sustain a relationship with them.

PERFECTIONISTS

Perfectionists can be difficult to spot. At first, they appear only as efficient, careful people who are effective and detail-oriented. To someone who hates detail and organization, that can be very appealing. But relationships, even love, are just

70

another area in need of control and regimentation to perfectionists. As a result, they are formal and stilted even with people close to them. New partners often expect perfectionists to relax once the relationship is established, but that rarely happens.

Luke and Sarah

Sarah was unpopular in school and considered herself unattractive, so she was surprised when Luke, a successful attorney, showed an interest in her. It must have been her intelligence and efficiency that attracted him. Being perfect and not making mistakes was her way to compensate for her feelings of inadequacy, and attention to details distracted her from anxieties about her appearance.

After fifteen years of marriage, Luke was fed up with Sarah's obsession with rules and limits, goals and timetables. Life with her was no fun. She was never spontaneous; everything had to be planned in advance. She was dull and boring and had few friends. She discussed minor matters to death and ignored the lack of pleasure in their lives.

Sarah couldn't let go of her perfectionistic tendencies even with their three children. As the children got older, she fought with their need to rebel. The fights between Sarah and their oldest daughter spread through the ranks, leaving Luke in the middle. He hated disciplining the children to appease her, but he couldn't tolerate the constant arguments.

Her attention to detail was maddening to him. She became enraged about the way the suitcases were packed for vacation. Once he was late picking her up after work because his car broke down. She didn't wait and took a bus home, then refused his apology and explanation when he finally arrived. If he had followed her car maintenance schedule, he wouldn't have car problems. The argument was long and bitter. That's when Luke decided he could no longer live with Sarah's restrictions.

* * *

To determine if your mate is a perfectionist, look for these traits:

- He or she has rules for everything, repeating them endlessly and pointing out infractions continually. Every rule has a rationale, discussed ad nauseam.

- Life is governed by timetables and schedules; spontaneity is forbidden.

- Trivial matters, like chores and errands, become obsessive. The goal is always accomplishment, never enjoyment.

- The need for perfection colors every decision because of the threat of mistakes. As a result, decisions often are not made.

BULLIES

Bullies are at the other end of the control freak continuum. Like perfectionists, they have rules and regulations. But they enforce them not with reason and explanation but with threats and intimidation. They use verbal and psychological abuse rather than violence, but the results are no less frightening and destructive.

Controlling others through intimidation and bullying is rarely a reversible behavior pattern. Typically, bullies have been raised in homes where such behavior was the norm. They may have powerful feelings of insecurity, inadequacy, and inferiority as a result of their childhood experiences and use their own behavior to hide their weaknesses.

Hugo and Irene

Hugo ruled his home with an iron fist. He had a horrible temper, which he considered his "buddy." Wherever he went, he brought his "buddy" to keep people in their place. He had a whole set of rules regarding his "buddy." If someone was disrespectful, arrogant, or antagonistic, his "buddy" might have to step in. His rages, when he felt crossed, humiliated, or threatened, were legendary.

The family caught the brunt of his temper. His eighteen-year-old daughter faced withering questions when she went out with her friends. Hugo's fourteen-year-old son got the third degree about schoolwork, athletics, and behavior. His wife, Irene, lived in terror. She dreaded the insults, demeaning comments, and continuous disrespect in front of the kids or company. To escape, she withdrew into her own world, caring only for her children. She was chronically nervous and developed physical symptoms of her anxiety, including stomach problems, headaches, and insomnia.

Hugo never hit his wife or the children, but all three circled him warily, expecting to be smacked at any moment. Intent on his own need to control, Hugo didn't realize his family told him only what they thought he wanted to hear or else avoided him.

After years of living on the edge, Irene decided to file for divorce. She claimed there was no special reason, she had just had it. Hugo, shocked, claimed to be unaware of Irene's feelings. He agreed to therapy and insisted he had no idea he had caused so much grief and fear in his own home.

He prided himself on his loyalty and dedication as a father and a husband. Therapy was very hard on Hugo, but he was able gradually to understand what Irene was feeling. He admitted that he didn't know how to make his wife and children love him; he knew only how to make them obey him. Over time, Hugo made significant changes in his attitudes and behavior, and Irene agreed to try again.

People who need to control without regard for another person's feelings and opinions are bullies. As with the mates of other rogues, spouses of bullies are not equal partners but the most available targets for their needs, whatever they may be.

They demand constant signs of obedience and respect, but acquiescence brings only temporary relief.

You can recognize bullies by the following traits:

- They make all the decisions about everything: your friends, what you wear, your finances, when you come and go, when you speak.

- They do not accept criticism. Whatever happened was your fault.

- Whenever their control is questioned, bullies unleash their temper.

- They are invariably jealous and possessive.

Any of the rogue lovers described above can be rescued, if they are willing to participate and work in therapy. A reluctant patient is less likely to change, however. Recognizing a behavior pattern can help you to make a decision and issue an ultimatum that may enforce the need to change.

A rogue who refuses to consider therapy is a hopeless case. So don't feel guilty about leaving the relationship. Often it is the only way to regain your self-esteem and confidence. It is much better to acknowledge the mistake and move on than to waste time and endanger your own sense of worth if you are involved with a rogue.

✦ 5

Futile Attractions

Futile attractions are just that—people who cannot sustain a healthy relationship. They are too involved in their own emotional needs and insecurities to be caring or even conscious of someone else.

Women or men who are involved with futile attractions often find escape very difficult. Usually, they have been subject to a form of brainwashing that has made them numb to their own needs. The dominant partner uses verbal, physical, and social humiliation to attack the mate, diminishing self-confidence, destroying self-esteem, and raising doubts about sensibility. The mate of a futile attraction is often a passive type to begin with, which the manipulator recognizes and exploits, knowing that even his or her worst behavior will not spark a confrontation.

Except in the extreme cases of physical abuse, many of those involved with futile attractions just need to understand how hopeless the situation is. Like the mates of rogue lovers, seeing their partner as typical of a problem personality, rather than unique and special, gives the lover of a futile attraction a more realistic idea of what to expect.

Knowing how precisely a mate's behavior follows a pattern suggests that the future will not be much different. This gives you the excuse to escape. There is no point in trying to reform someone who refuses to realize the need for change.

EGOTISTS

The egotist excites more voyeuristic interest than virtually any other rogue. Most of us have at times fantasized what it would be like to act solely from self-interest. Countless movies and books have recounted the story of the selfish, self-absorbed character who pursues self-interest with little regard for others—Larry Hagman's J. R. Ewing on the hit series *Dallas* is a good example.

Egotists are not always immediately apparent. In a new relationship, they often mask their self-absorption by showing a seemingly genuine concern. But the facade fades quickly and their overwhelming selfishness is not far below the surface.

Eventually, most people involved with egotists realize that they don't care about anyone else. It's like the old joke about the actor who meets an old friend and talks for ten minutes about his work, then says, "Enough about me. Let's talk about you. What did you think about my latest role?"

Andy and Nora

As a computer software salesman and consultant, Andy had erratic working hours and didn't keep to any schedule. He liked to spend time with his friends and always had a deal or a game working. His interests took priority, just as his expensive hobbies ate up most of his money. Nora, his wife, captured his attention only when she did something wrong, which was most of the time. He condescendingly talked about her faults and limitations, never bothered to notify her of a change in plans, and carried on affairs with other women.

Nora didn't work steadily because of Andy's erratic schedule. Her part-time job as an office assistant paid little, and she became more and more dependent on him. He, in turn, expected her to keep his life running smoothly, paying bills and doing the chores and everything else. He wanted to come and go as he wished, sure of what was waiting when he finally walked in the door.

When one of his deals fell through or his business did poorly, he expected Nora to help him pick up the pieces. In between, he blamed her for their failing marriage. She was too clingy and dependent. Her weakness and insecurity held him back. Her poor-paying, low-status job was proof of her timidity and the reason he didn't spend more time with her.

Disinterested in anyone else's needs, egotists lack empathy for others. They are usually success driven, and material goods are proof of their importance.

Like Andy, egotists love control and criticize what they can't dominate. They cannot tolerate criticism, disapproval, or rejection. Since their personal needs are the only criteria, they act irresponsibly. Relationships and commitments are of no consequence. Neither are people, unless they can provide the attention, approval, and admiration egotists need.

Egotists love control and avoid situations they can't dominate. Thus they want a totally dependent mate. They will alienate you from friends and family so that nothing distracts you from meeting their needs.

SEXUALLY INCOMPATIBLES

Even in the 1990s coming out and admitting homosexuality is fraught with fears and risks that not all gay men and lesbians are willing to assume. For some, there is the social pressure from family, friends, and coworkers. For others, there are the risks of adopting an alternative lifestyle—everything from random violence to AIDS and other sexually transmitted diseases.

Many homosexuals put off the anguish associated with disclosure for as long as possible. Others secretly hope to pass as straight so that they can pursue a career or have children. Unfortunately for the partners they choose, the prospects for an honest, intimate relationship are poor.

Simon and Jennifer

Simon met Jennifer when he was in his early twenties. They developed a close relationship, but Simon had lots of vague excuses for postponing marriage. He wasn't sure if he wanted to be married. He was concerned how his burgeoning political career might affect their relationship. He wanted to be successful at the small accounting firm he inherited from his father. Jennifer agreed to wait.

During the next five years, there were many times when Jennifer almost discovered Simon's secret, but he always managed to come up with an explanation for his unusual behavior. Once, she attended a political convention with him. Late one night, he left the room, supposedly going for a nightcap. Jennifer decided to join him and went down to the bar, but Simon wasn't there. When Jennifer couldn't find him anywhere else, she called an acquaintance of his also attending the convention. Simon was in the room. Later he explained that he had decided—at one in the morning—to talk with his old friend about the next day's agenda.

Jennifer was uneasy with that explanation and several similar incidents, but she never suspected that Simon was gay. He had a reputation for being honest, trustworthy, and devoted to helping others. He was popular in the community and had excellent prospects for election to a state office. He wanted children and insisted that he loved Jennifer.

They got married, and for a while everything seemed fine. But Simon found himself filled with guilt and remorse from his deceptions and infidelity. Jennifer suspected that something was amiss, since he frequently seemed on edge and his behavior was erratic. She wondered if he was having an affair, but there were many signs that belied that assumption. Simon was always thoughtful, and his character was impeccable. He showed no interest in women and seemed interested only in his work and politics.

It was easy for her to accept that he was working late and

that work-related problems frequently arose because of his political involvement. As time went on, his guilt increased. Jennifer was too insecure and dependent on him to question his increasingly erratic behavior. Even when he disappeared at night, returning very late with some almost reasonable explanation, she barely voiced a question. Simon also had difficulty asserting himself and was confused about his sexual identity.

Their sex life together was nonexistent and Jennifer felt rejected. She lost confidence in herself. Hoping to make the marriage work, she overlooked his choice of friends and his late nights. Her friends had urged counseling before they married, but she had rejected the advice. During the marriage, she still refused to confront the problems, fearing further rejection.

Eventually Simon realized that he could not keep up the charade. When Jennifer learned the truth, she was heartbroken. She tried to work things out, but Simon was unable to live with the conditions she requested. She insisted that he end his homosexual involvements. He refused, confessing that his feelings for her were more intellectual than emotional. He saw her as a good friend and partner, not a lover.

Some gay men manage to deceive their wives for many years. They even appear to have a successful marriage. But once the woman discovers the truth—and she does eventually—the relationship is typically shattered. Looking back, the woman recognizes the intricate set of lies and denials and concludes that she cannot trust her partner.

Although a reconciliation is, in theory, possible, most women can't allow their mates to continue having sexual relations with men. Nor are both partners willing to accept celibacy. As a result, most therapists openly acknowledge the futility of reconciliation and try to avoid fostering unrealistic expectations.

There are typical signals that your partner is gay:

- Your sexual meetings are few and far between, or nonexistent.

- He/she is frequently away from home and secretive about how that time is spent.

- He/she is not particularly interested in the opposite sex, so you develop a false sense of security.

- He/she is usually responsible and affectionate with the children, but not with you.

PERPETUAL ADOLESCENTS

Many therapists believe that American men don't lose the last vestiges of adolescence until thirtysomething. And many wives have testified to the accuracy of the adage, "The only difference between men and boys is the price of their toys." For most of us, the need to earn a living and the arrival of children establish limits of responsibility and conduct that preclude a prolonged childhood.

But not for all. Some men can't let go of their youth. Anything that smacks of adulthood or restraints sends them flying in the opposite direction. Since they won't consider the future—or the past, which implies aging—the present is their only focus and their only aim is to have a good time.

Bridget and Patrick

Patrick was a ski instructor who met Bridget while she was vacationing with her husband. The good-looking ski buff was the exact opposite of her formal, overbearing, insensitive, overly independent, serious, humorless husband. Patrick was all fun and impulsiveness, quick to laugh, a good athlete, humorous, energetic, and imaginative.

As Bridget spent more time with him, she was taken with his carefree nature. Patrick was always up for excitement and never complained about anything except people who tried to put a damper on his life. He always had a good time wherever he was. Nothing affected his sunny mood.

Patrick insisted that his intense love for Bridget would last, and he wanted her to get a divorce so they could marry. Bridget gave some serious thought to leaving her husband. But Patrick worked sporadically, as a ski instructor in the winter and at a surfing shop in the summer. He had no savings. He showed no interest in Bridget's twelve-year-old daughter beyond asking her favorite sport. It seemed that all he liked to do was party and travel.

On the other hand, her husband was responsible, a good provider, of good character, and highly moral. Bridget decided to stop seeing Patrick and pursue marital therapy with her husband.

Lana and Charles

Lana, an extremely attractive fashion designer, is successful, bright, and articulate. Her wardrobe reflects her taste and professionalism. She exercises regularly and watches her diet. She has an upbeat personality and an optimistic outlook on life. She's a well-organized, responsible woman who gets along well with her many friends and coworkers.

Lana's boyfriend, Charles, was her polar opposite. He smoked two packs of cigarettes a day. His ill-fitting clothes were odd combinations of colors and patterns that didn't match. He showed no interest in his appearance. Even Lana recognized the incongruity of their pairing, but he seemed unaware. He was self-assured and confident.

In therapy sessions, Lana confirmed my suspicions about Charles. He hated work and avoided any responsibility. He lived with his parents and worked the occasional odd jobs. He slept most of the day and prowled all night. He indulged himself with alcohol, women, and junk-food binges. When he had money, as he did from an inheritance after his grandmother's death, he spent it without regard to savings. He lived for the moment and showed no interest in planning for or anticipating the future.

Although everyone in town knew and greeted him, Charles had no real friends. He didn't get on well with his father, who nevertheless supported him. He drank too much, smoked too much, and refused to bathe regularly. He was charming but moody, often lost in his own world.

Lana was aware of what she described as quirks, but she thought his good points outweighed them. Even though he took advantage of any opportunity to stray, he always came back. He didn't seek out women, but if they approached him, he didn't resist. He was charming and brilliant, and he was willing to play private to Lana's general.

Lana's view of marriage was colored by her own childhood. Her parents, both professionals, had related as friends. They divorced when she left for college. Looking back it was obvious that they stayed together for her and her sister. Her parents had rarely argued and they seemed to get along, but now, Lana realized, they had just been going through the motions. Charles represented the opposite. He was very much in love with her and expressed his care and concern without embarrassment. When she came to his house, he would prepare an elaborate meal, fussing over details. He always had a good bottle of wine and set an exquisite table.

Their conversations were interesting and charged. Charles spoke on a wide range of topics with considerable insight and knowledge, gained from spending hours watching CNN and reading books and newspapers. He had a distinctly personal perspective on events and the people they knew. He also had an uncanny knack for predicting people's decisions and figuring out things most people didn't notice.

Whenever Lana had time, Charles was available. She liked looking after him. She nurtured and fussed over him, bragging about her successes, such as getting him to eat less junk food and take vitamins. Taking care of his tax returns and applying for his education grant was a labor of love for Lana.

Then Charles's father died and he was forced to find a job to support himself. Charles put Lana to the test, saying he planned to move to Florida to work for his brother since he couldn't find work in the area. He hated to leave her, but he had no other option. She saw his threatened move as an ultimatum: Either you support me until I am able to find work, however long that may be, or I'm leaving. Lana was willing to go only so far, and that did not include supporting him.

Lana let him go. She was heartbroken, but she realized he wasn't just asking for help; he wanted a meal ticket. She needed more from a relationship than Charles had to offer.

The perpetual adolescent acts as if he doesn't have a care in the world. He gives the impression that he loves life, enjoys getting together with his buddies, and doesn't concern himself with the fact that his life is woefully underdeveloped. But he has strong underlying feelings of anxiety, which are the reasons for his behavior. He is an underachiever, too afraid of failure and humiliation even to try. If he never accepts responsible behavior he can't be condemned for not succeeding at anything. He maintains a mask of invulnerability and indifference to his lack of achievement.

The adolescent is capable of commitment, but once married acts as if he is still single. He spends free time with buddies, not family. He relates to his children as a playmate, not a parent. He may talk about the need to change but resists it at all costs. His life moves from crisis to crisis—financial problems are common, as are infidelity and alcoholism. When depressed—after losing a job or faced with financial problems—he talks convincingly of change but always returns to his old ways once the crisis passes.

This boyish man often attracts strong, nurturing women who want to take care of him. Or else he chooses a passive woman who won't complain about his lack of ambition and achievement. Both kinds of partners spend a lot of time mothering their perpetual adolescent—cleaning up messes, soothing hurts, nagging about bad habits, and providing assurances of love and affection.

Adolescents, whether adults or teenagers, act impulsively. They don't plan. They are poor bets for the long haul because they refuse to be equal partners. Individually, many of the characteristics of the perpetual adolescent are charming, but they take a darker perspective when seen as part of an established pattern.

MR. EXCITEMENT

Mr. Excitement is always trying something new, looking for the rush of novelty and excitement. He likes to party and meet new people. He is fun to be with, spontaneous, and seemingly unpredictable. But he follows patterns no less rigid than those of other futile attractions, and he is no more hopeful as a permanent partner.

Meg and Dan

Meg, twenty-six, was the youngest of five children. Her parents just squeaked by financially so she got only hand-me-downs. Hardly anything she ever had was hers entirely, and she longed to be on her own. Her father was verbally and physically abusive, and her mother was a passive-dependent who was unable to protect her.

She was close to her second brother, who was warm and agreeable and seemed to accept her as she was. Meg avoided her oldest brother and felt alienated to a lesser degree from the rest of her family. Looking back, she felt she never developed a sense of identity or security while growing up. She remembered fantasizing about someone who would truly love her and whisk her away.

Dan, twenty-eight, was the embodiment of charm and confidence. Nothing was beyond his reach. Everything was doable; just ask and he'd arrange it. He loved adventure and excitement and had lots of money and tons of friends. Everybody in town knew him; he always had a funny story to relate. He loved to laugh and did not have a bad word for anyone—except for a few people, especially his parents, who let him down—"But don't ask since there is no sense worrying about that. . . . I can get by without them."

Loyalty was everything, according to Dan. He expressed his need for trust and allegiance loudly and often: "I'd never let a friend down, no matter what he did, even if I had to go against the law or whatever. As far as I'm concerned, you stick by your friends, period."

Dan bolstered Meg's self-esteem and confidence. He encouraged her to be independent and told her how much he depended on her and loved her. In his eyes, she was beautiful, and he had no problem telling her so. He was devoted and committed to her and would stand by her through all circumstances. He was everything that Meg had longed for. Whatever she wanted he was happy to oblige. He gave her all the freedom she wanted and asked only for her loyalty.

He enrolled in a GED program and breezed through it. Meg was thrilled and looked forward to better days. Dan started his own business as a roofer. One day, he fell off a roof, hurting his back and dislocating his shoulder. Meg was sympathetic and took a second job to help out.

During the six months he was unemployed, Dan helped around the house, did some chores, and made a few dollars playing with a local band. Most of the household chores, however, fell on Meg, who also did all the shopping, cooked the meals, and paid the bills. She was exhausted, but she dutifully listened every night to his complaints about jerks who wouldn't hire the rock bands he was always putting together or his wild schemes to turn things around.

Dan finally started a business repairing appliances, but the work was infrequent and he was financially dependent on Meg. He spent his days hanging out at home and his nights with friends. He assured Meg that things would work out and asked for her patience and loyalty.

One night, after stopping for a beer with a friend, Dan was spotted speeding by the police. He tried to lose them but got caught. He was convicted of drunk driving and lost his license for two years. Meg had to borrow several thousand dollars from her family to pay his legal fees. She also found herself chauffeuring Dan all over town. Sometimes he drove to see his friends or to a bar, not worrying about being caught because, "I have a friend on the force who'll get me out, and I could always outrun the police."

Meg had grown weary of all of Dan's setbacks and began to question his excuses. He turned the tables on her and accused her of being like all the rest: "No one ever helps me. I always have to do everything myself. I wish I were out of here. I thought of ending it before, and that's the only way. . . . Don't worry, I won't be here when you get back. I don't want your help anymore."

Meg felt sick with guilt and tried to rally Dan's support. She went to see his parents, who told her to leave him. They had long ago broken off contact because he was always irresponsible and dishonest. They described him as a hopeless con artist. Meg began to suspect that Dan had told her innumerable lies that were beginning to catch up with him. His parents were actually very nice and seemed sincerely interested in helping her.

According to his family, Dan avoided work and took advantage of people. He often ended up draining them of all the money they would give him. He was incredibly good at making people feel guilty and obligated to him.

Meg was shocked, but she was forced to admit that everything they said was true. She was devastated and sought out people who might know a different side of him. But she found only more lies. Dan had used different stories to borrow money from her friends. He got cash from his friends by saying that Meg never helped him. He had had numerous affairs during their marriage. He had a different excuse for everyone about why his business had failed.

Meg said, "I never loved someone so much, and I don't think I ever will. He was perfect, except for the problems that kept coming up. Whenever we would get through some fix, something else would pop up. It was incredible. It always seemed that we just had to get over this one last obstacle and we'd be free, but it never happened. And then one day I realized it would never end. After a while, I couldn't eat, and I lost about fifteen pounds. That's when I realized I couldn't go on. I felt incredibly guilty for letting him down; it was the only thing he ever asked of me."

It's difficult not to feel guilty when you finally decide to walk out on Mr. Excitement. Women also commonly report feeling incredibly stupid and angry once they are free. The illusion of love and devotion may last long after the facts are in. Often family and friends see through the con well before the victim does.

In fact, most people can't imagine how the victim fell for his obvious lies. But Mr. Excitement is adept at uncovering and apparently fulfilling his victim's emotional needs. Dan also had sociopathic tendencies. This is not always the case, although it is not uncommon in this type.

After a while, the constant quest for excitement becomes boring. A woman who originally was attracted to the spontaneity and impulsiveness now longs for stability and security. She has become worn down by the nonstop action, the buddies—obvious losers—who are always hanging around, the late nights, the cigarettes and alcohol.

The relationship often ends with a disaster. In many cases, he dies or you do. Or he gets arrested or you both do. Or medical problems overwhelm one of you.

If you leave, he will try to win you back, making his usual extravagant promises. But as with everything else, he is easily distracted and soon gives up. You don't have to stay just because you love him, especially if he is endangering the children or keeping you trapped in a marriage that isn't growing.

Individuals have different energy levels, discernible almost from birth. Even in the nursery, infants show varying levels of activity that continue throughout life. A person whose energy is slightly above average is fun to be with. But when the energy level gets too high, he may be unable to control his impulses. A person with a very high energy level who exhibits the tendencies listed below is a poor risk in a relationship:

- He loves excitement and cannot feel low levels of arousal. In order to experience anything, it must be an intense rush. Real life is boring and he has to generate excitement to feel good.

- He loves to play brinkmanship, last-minute or eleventh-hour scenes are the norm.

- His conscience is poorly formed. Lying and cheating increase the excitement.

- He has trouble focusing on the present. It's always "Let's get out of here. Let's go." He loves to talk about what is coming up, the next big one, the next gig. The next one is always anticipated more than it is enjoyed.

- He loves to travel, start anew, change plans, discuss and plot strategies.

- He has difficulty holding onto money. Usually money comes and goes in bursts. He makes a killing and spends it fast, then he muddles through on your money until the next quick fix.

SOCIOPATHS

Sociopaths are people without a conscience. Many of them become violent career criminals. But other sociopaths, usually after a youthful experience with the justice system, opt for a less flamboyant path. They avoid violence for the most part, relying instead on their ability to manipulate, lie, and distract.

Research indicates that 3 percent of the male population and 1 percent of all women are sociopaths. The behavior pattern becomes apparent early, often before adolescence. Children with a history of school problems, truancy, fights, and lying are prime candidates. Such troubled youngsters are often daredevils in street play, become sexually active at an early age, and experiment with drugs and alcohol. They have difficulty establishing friendships, and they don't seem to learn from their mistakes. As teenagers, they demonstrate a marked amorality and callousness toward others. They rarely complete high school.

Sue and Tomas

Sue was thirtysomething, never married, when Tomas called her. They had met a few years earlier when she was the creative director on an ad campaign for a drug program where he worked. He was a consultant, introduced as someone who had gone through the program years earlier and since had gone on to graduate from college and become a certified counselor.

They started dating, and Sue found herself somewhat overwhelmed by his wealth of stories and experiences. An assertive career woman, she was fascinated by his street smarts, flattered by his affection, and reassured by the admiration of his colleagues. His apparent ambition and courage in the face of overwhelming odds were attractive.

Her friends were amazed when she announced their engagement, but the wedding took place less than a year after Tomas's first phone call. He had left the job at the drug program long before and was now working with an activist lawyer. Sue earned a lot more money, so he had moved into her apartment, but that was temporary. His earnings would buy them a vacation house in the Caribbean, he promised.

Within a few months, Tomas was no longer working for the lawyer, although Sue never quite understood what happened. He went through a series of jobs, quitting each for something that always looked better but never came through. He tried driving a cab for a while, using Sue's money to buy a used car. He had claimed to be an old hot-rodder, but the car he bought was a lemon that cost more to fix than it ever earned for him.

As time passed, Sue began to see a pattern emerging. Tomas had no money of his own. He never held a job. He was always talking about some big scheme, but it was always a few months away, by which time Tomas was on to something else. He told the same Vietnam stories over and over, and Sue began to notice the inconsistencies. Sometimes she pointed them out, and he would offer some involved, complex explanation that never made sense.

The turning point came when Sue lost her job. Tomas decided to buy an ounce of cocaine to sell at a profit. When he showed up with the drugs, she was furious. She asked where he got the money, and he told some story about an old friend and an odd job. She insisted he get rid of the cocaine. Instead, Tomas headed for the Caribbean to make his killing. After he left, Sue realized that money was missing from her savings account, just enough for an ounce of cocaine and a trip to the islands.

Sue filed for divorce. She was angry with herself for giving him access to her bank card and personal code when she had already begun to distrust him. After the divorce, she learned that his whole history was false. He had not been in the drug program, he had never gone to college, he had never served in Vietnam.

Sociopaths show an early pattern of destroyed trust and wrecked relationships. Usually boys from dysfunctional homes, they lead the playground in heedless behavior. They are insensitive, exploitative, delinquent, and often very calculating. From childhood on, they show no regard for anyone else. They act to meet their immediate needs, whatever they may be, without regard for long-term consequences, effects, or results.

Because he has no conscience, a sociopath will never change and cannot be trusted when he promises he will. He shows extraordinary ability to fake remorse and guilt but doesn't hesitate to repeat the behavior. If he's miserable to live with and impossible to change, the only alternative is to leave. If your mate shows the traits listed below, start looking for new quarters:

- He shows no conscience, guilt, morality, or allegiance to anyone or anything.

- He has long and complex explanations for every apparent lapse. Because he is so adept at reading people and manipulating them, it may take a long time for his true nature to be apparent.

- He is totally irresponsible.

- He regularly abuses everything—drugs, alcohol, tobacco, caffeine, sugar, junk food, and people. Without a conscience, he has no restraints on what he will do or say.

BRUTES

Some men feel so threatened that they lash out at everything, especially whatever is closest. That's usually the women in their lives. Brutes are wife-beaters and usually child-beaters as well, often because that's how they were treated as children.

Fred and Sarah

Sarah, thirty-six, worked as a nurse in a cardiologist's office. She had divorced the moody guy she married after college. For ten years, she tried to cure him, but finally she got tired of the boredom, negativity, lack of ambition, and pessimism.

Fred was the opposite: energetic, optimistic, enthusiastic, and upbeat. They were married within a year.

Fred was irreverent, confident in his street smarts and his ideas. He overestimated his own abilities and underestimated everyone else's. After they were married, his past kept catching up with him. He was arrested twice for failing to pay out-of-state tickets. He was charged with failing to pay child support. When he resisted arrest, assault was added to the charges. He couldn't keep a job and borrowed money from Sarah.

Afraid Sarah would leave him now that she recognized how inadequate he was, he tried to control the relationship. He joked about her naïveté and mocked her career and the office where she worked. He argued with friends and family, who stopped seeing them. He played with martial-arts weapons, boasting of his lethal skills and intimidating her with his threat of violence. He told Sarah he would kill anyone who showed an interest in her, and he'd maim her if she tried to leave him.

Fred became more depressed and abusive as his debts mounted and he was unable to find a job. One day, he hit Sarah for talking to a man in their apartment complex. He was remorseful, then hit her again when she nagged him about drinking all day and not looking for a job. Then he hit her for nagging him about using her car. Eventually, he was hitting her almost every day. He refused to discuss any problems and used silence and anger to thwart her attempts to work out their troubles.

Although she had a well-paying job, Sarah felt trapped. She was afraid that Fred would injure or even kill her if she left him. Although he monitored the money, she managed to set aside a little each week. After a year, she had saved $1,500 and was able to get her own apartment. She made sure to notify the police and get a restraining order against Fred. She also entered a program for battered women to get additional support. Once she was really free, she experienced an enormous sense of relief. It made her realize how much of an ordeal her life with Fred had been.

Brutes are at the extreme of behavior. They are dangerous and life-threatening. A man who beats a woman keeps beating her until she is dead or he goes to jail. It is one of the most common—and underreported—crimes in the United States.

Because abusers usually choose passive women and keep them isolated, it is often difficult for the victims to get away. Thousands of women die each year at the hands of men who promised to love them. Shelters for battered women are found in most large cities. The woman often leaves with only the clothes on her back, but once she finds a haven, she is protected from further contact with her abuser.

In many relationships, the abuse eventually brings the police. But then the woman must agree to press charges and not back down. That can be difficult for a woman who has been beaten and humiliated for years. Some cities now require overnight incarceration of abusive men, and many provide counseling as well. But therapy won't work unless the brute wants to change. That usually requires ultimatums from a judge as well as the woman.

All futile attractions can make life miserable, but a brute can kill you. A man who hits you once rarely stops there. If the following characteristics describe your partner or your relationship, you need to get help:

- He abuses you physically—or verbally and emotionally.

- He structures the household with rigid controls, orders, and commands.

- He controls the money.

- He isolates you from your family and friends.

- He loses control during rages; you can't predict how far he will go.

- You are frightened all or most of the time.

The futile attractions in this chapter and the rogues in the previous one are impossibly difficult to live with. Their deep-seated fears and excessive needs dominate the lives of everyone they touch. They maintain their masks with lies, manipulation, intimidation, and threats. They are uniformly selfish, irresponsible, untrustworthy, and dishonest. Those who love them are invariably subjected to abuse, humiliation, financial insecurity, and loss of friends and family.

If the past chapters have described your marriage or affair, it is time honestly to analyze your life and your future. The next chapter will help you understand the nature of your relationship and what to do to break free. If you decide that your partner is a hopeless case and you want to get out before it's too late, the next section provides explanations, tactics, strategies, and thinking patterns that will help.

Falling out of love, even with a hopeless case, is not easy. But it is possible.

6

Ambivalence and Desensitization

Uncertainty and Anxiety

𝒩ow that you are seeing your partner or relationship more clearly, the next step is to consider the future.
If you've decided to end the relationship or you find yourself
alone through death or an unwanted separation, the next few
months will be difficult and challenging. You will experience
complicated feelings, not all of them comfortable.

The next few chapters untangle those feelings and suggest
ways to face up to them and put them to use. First I explain
some of the feelings people face when they are trying to make
the break in a relationship, how uncertainty, ambivalence,
and anxiety are techniques that have evolved to help you. I
also provide some suggestions for lessening the intensity of
any uncomfortable experience. The last chapter focuses on
people who find themselves unexpectedly bereft of a partner.
Whatever the reasons for abandonment, the emotions evoked
are similar.

The stages of ending a relationship are similar to those for
any expected loss: a series of mental survival tactics every bit
as strong as the fight-or-flight response to a threat.

People are usually trapped by psychological fears rather
than situational handicaps. But even if you believe that your
special situation—a sick child, personal disability, financial
dependence, etc.—makes separation impossible, learning
more about the process can open doors you didn't know
about and provide an escape. The techniques are effective.

Early humankind developed responses to many primitive
threats. Grief, the human response to loss, was a ritual that

helped keep the community together. How the tribe reacted when a member was missing or lost—did it conduct a brief, perfunctory search? or did it look and look, not giving up until all hope was lost?—probably determined whether the tribe survived. If the searches were quickly abandoned, the message was that members weren't very important, they didn't matter. Spirit and morale, qualities vital to human survival and success, would be undermined. But if the search went on and on, tirelessly (within some reasonable limits, of course), a healthy we-count, we-matter camaraderie was formed.

The grief reaction helped to keep the group together, working for the benefit of all. It also helped individuals learn from losses to avoid further grief. Those may be the most important guides for survival we get in a lifetime. The human need to make bad times better often provides the spur to make changes, adopt new tactics, try new strategies.

All important losses bring feelings of grief, loss, anxiety, and uncertainty for individuals. Just anticipating the end of an important relationship evokes those negative and painful emotions before the fact. The expectation of sure emotional anguish may make us draw back from taking action, thus postponing these frightening, uncomfortable, and disturbing feelings.

Often, people facing difficult situations are ambivalent, unable even to think about decisions without feeling panicky. The emotional turmoil makes them feel as if they are losing control, so they avoid any dangerous areas. It will help if you recognize that the uncertainty—the ambivalence—is part of the process. The mind repetitiously contemplates the loss, considering ways to prevent it, figuring how to adapt to it, weighing methods of reversing it, and choosing alternatives to compensate for it. The process also allows a person to become enured to the loss over a period of time.

In my experience, ambivalence is the first phase of the mind's response to a difficult choice that will end in a loss. It doesn't matter if the choices offer real alternatives or if one option is much more attractive than the other; the process allows you to consider both of them. Ambivalence—the shift in focus on each alternative in turn until the mind gradually becomes desensitized to the evoked anxieties for either choice—provides breathing room, a period to cool off and approach the problem with less emotion.

Each time you consider one alternative, the emotions brought on by losing the other choice are similar to a depressive reaction, causing anxiety and other negative feelings. The usual response is to change directions and consider the second possibility. That in turn brings up feelings of loss for the first alternative. Staying with an unfaithful partner, for example, means losing independence and self-esteem. Going off on your own means losing the security and history of a developed partnership.

That is the ambivalence process. It allows you gradually to desensitize the anxieties associated with the loss of each alternative. Usually, you start by imagining the positive results of one choice, then bring up the negative feelings. When the sense of loss and sadness becomes overwhelming, you switch to the alternative—no loss, just the pluses of this choice until you recall what you're losing by giving up the other. In this way, you gradually become accustomed to the idea of losing one option.

When first confronted with this kind of a decision, the ambivalence is rapid. Several times a day, the choices will reverse themselves because the pain of either loss seems unbearable. These thoughts are fleeting at first, the pain so great that the mind looks for immediate distractions. Gradually, the alternatives are considered for longer and longer periods as the anxieties associated with each become more familiar and less painful.

This lessening of pain is called desensitization. It works in your mind the way a callus works on your hand, allowing you to do hard, dirty work without causing lasting damage. The more frequently you consider painful choices and the longer you analyze the evoked anxieties, the less disturbing they become. Familiarity may not breed contempt, but it reduces fear.

As ambivalence desensitizes the anxieties associated with both of your choices, it gives you more time to consider them and to decide which option is truly the best. It reduces the fear of loss as the mind gradually ponders each alternative in turn. Ambivalence provides you with the opportunity to analyze each choice in detail and to look at the related issues.

The ambivalence process is subject to some complications that can hide its effectiveness. The mind prioritizes issues based on their importance to our survival, reflected in their emotional intensity. That is, it focuses on the problem with the highest emotional content until that level drops in relation to other issues. Then the focus goes to the situation with the new highest emotional response. Until the anxiety levels of every issue are reduced, it may be difficult to recognize that any progress has been made.

Suppose you are faced with leaving an abusive partner but are afraid to face life on your own. As you vacillate, ambivalent about your alternatives, you will consider a number of individual problems: What about the kids? What about money? How can I change his behavior? What am I doing wrong? Assuming that each of these has an anxiety level of eight on a ten-point scale, you will feel overwhelmed.

As you consider solutions to each one and become desensitized, the anxiety level for the issue you have focused on may drop to four. Then you look at the next issue, which is at level eight. That gives you the impression that you're not making any progress and may bring on a sense of futility. The progress doesn't become apparent until you consider all the issues and desensitize them below the initial level of eight.

In this case, you may try to think of ways to appease the abuser so you can stay in the familiar relationship. When your fear of staying becomes overwhelming, you'll think about leaving until the problems of money, independence, and loneliness seem unbearable. As each alternative gains favor, you consider answers to the problems of losing the other, desensitizing each anxiety and providing potential solutions to the situation.

For many women, this scenario is complicated by feelings of low self-esteem and concerns about support and escape. Abusive people isolate their partners, cutting them off from friends and family. Often, years of ridicule and humiliation have given the abused person a distorted image of herself and the world around her. In such instances, the ambivalence comes from a lack of self-confidence, not the pull of two equally attractive choices.

Faced with an impossible situation, but hesitant to escape, women often blame themselves and see the uncertainty and vacillation of the ambivalence process as proof of their inadequacy and inability to live apart from the brutal partner. They understand the danger and are disgusted with their inability to act. As a result, they become more fearful and uncertain, unable to stay where they are and doubtful of their ability to get away.

Molly

Caring for a three-year-old son with severe asthma and a nine-year-old daughter, Molly felt trapped in a futile marriage. Her husband taunted her with his lack of interest, parading his lovers and disappearing on a whim. The demands of the children made working impossible, so Molly never considered leaving—it was a waste of time to even consider it.

In therapy, Molly began to indulge her thoughts of leaving. Once she started to explore, she discovered that day care and community-shared child care were available. She could work part-time. A support group further enhanced her self-esteem.

Molly learned that her own sense of futility played into her husband's lack of respect. That in turn increased her fears and lowered her self-esteem, leading to more disrespect from her husband. Once she broke the circle, using ambivalence to face her fears, they diminished. Her actions on her own behalf prompted her husband to treat her better, and her marriage improved.

People often use their special circumstances as an excuse to avoid thinking about ending an abusive or impossible relationship. But that attitude only makes the situation worse. When you consider yourself trapped, others reach the same conclusion and treat you accordingly. Knowing you do not have to tolerate abuse is the best protection against it. Abusers have no respect for their victims. It is only when you stand up for yourself that you can end the abuse, or get rid of the abuser.

It helps if you understand that the ambivalence process is a strategy developed by the mind to help you make difficult decisions. The ambivalent feelings encourage you to consider each alternative carefully. Once you appreciate how this process works, it is easier for you to face the hesitancy and uncertainty and use them to your advantage.

In general, the mind focuses on the issue closest to survival. If you are having an important conversation with your lover, your mind will note, but ignore, the hiss of an air conditioner. But if the hiss comes from a rattlesnake, your lover rapidly fades into the background as you confront this immediate threat to your survival.

Left to itself, the mind concentrates on priority needs until they are met. You can divert your attention for short periods, deciding not to think about your relationship at work, for example. If you don't distract yourself constantly, the mind wanders back to its more important priorities—the problems at home.

The ambivalence process is frustrating to people who are used to making decisions and choices without difficulty.

They confuse ambivalence with indecisiveness, a negative character trait associated with incompetence, poor mental skills, poor character, weak personality, and cowardice. Indecisiveness is a lifelong characteristic that colors every choice. Ambivalence is a process for reducing anxiety when confronted with life-changing choices between two incompatible alternatives.

Nevertheless, many people find ambivalence intolerable and try to regulate their attention, refusing to consider the options they are facing. This doesn't work. It requires strong will power and unflagging attention, exhausting mental and even physical energy, to avoid thinking about problems the mind considers serious or even threatening. As a result, the person trying to escape that process is often less effective at work or around the house.

By ignoring the ambivalence process, you lose the chance to become desensitized to fears and free-floating anxieties. You can't solve your current dilemma and you can't lessen your anxiety level, so you feel inept. Since you distract your attention, you don't have the opportunity to consider the merits of each issue, but you continue to feel the anxiety evoked when your attention strays. Some people get so upset at their seeming inability to make major decisions that they turn off their thinking, refusing to look at any problems. One man boasted that he parked his mind in the trunk and felt better for it.

Ambivalence is a highly sophisticated and elegant means of resolving a seemingly irreconcilable problem. Indecisiveness, by contrast, is the inability to arrive at a decision because of any number of factors, including poor motivation, depression, lack of information, and poor leadership skills.

When people used to making decisions face the ambivalence process, they may misinterpret it. Often they take some kind of action just to prove they are not weak-minded. They may make a major purchase as evidence that they have reached a decision and are locked into that choice. For example, a single man thinking about a new live-in partner may make an addition to his house as proof of his commitment before he issues an invitation.

George

At thirty-four, George worked in the family business in the garment industry. He considered himself a successful, self-assured executive who regularly made tough business decisions. Yet when he first considered leaving his wife for another woman, he felt overwhelmed by anxiety. Rather than face the anguish of his uncertainty, he made a quick, clean break.

Once he was out of the house, he realized how emotionally wrenching his actions were. He'd left a wife and two children, and his sense of guilt and responsibility dazed him. Pride and self-image made it difficult to admit his confusion and doubts. Unused to uncertainty, he entered therapy, convinced he was going insane.

By accepting ambivalence as a natural process that he could use to his advantage, he stopped running from the emotional turmoil. Once he began thinking objectively about his alternatives, he realized that he was blinded by his girlfriend's beauty and his wife's weight problems. He also recognized that he had never discussed her weight with his wife because he didn't want her to know he disliked it. A frank discussion brought important changes at home and George broke up with his girlfriend, determined to give his marriage a chance.

Lloyd

A forty-one-year-old computer executive, Lloyd saw life as a competition, and he was determined to win. He was especially determined that no woman, particularly his wife, would get the better of him.

When she divorced him, he directed all of his attention to undermining her financial security. He never considered the interests of his children and how he could help them adjust to the divorce, or whether he still loved his wife. He threatened to quit his job and lock away his pension. He swore that she would never be free of him, never able to date another man. He talked of scaring off her boyfriends, calling her employer, damaging her car, alienating her friends.

In therapy he learned to confront all of his fears. It helped him to understand why the marriage had failed and enabled him to let go despite his fear of losing.

Although there is no way to avoid the ambivalence process when you are faced with a difficult choice between two seemingly incompatible alternatives, there are ways to manage the anxiety and depression that you are feeling. First of all, just knowing that anxiety and depression are natural, expected results can be helpful. Understanding the process and recognizing the pattern provide reassurance that your feelings of anxiety, uncertainty, and even panic are not uncommon. Further, they can be directed, if not completely controlled. You can learn to work with those feelings, not fight the natural flow of emotion, reaction, and even regression.

Ellen and Joel

Joel was subject to wild mood swings, frequently erupting in abusive anger toward Ellen. Although he was warm and endearing at other times, she was constantly alert for his changes. She was exhausted by his instability and wanted to leave, but she was concerned about her financial security if she did. Afraid to take the chance on her own, she stayed with him for years, vacillating between the alternatives of moving out or continuing as they were.

During those years, Ellen assumed that her ambivalence was evidence of her own weakness and low self-esteem, so she continually distracted herself, further reducing her ability to take action. Once she began therapy and learned that the ambivalence was a normal process, she became more self-confident. She felt reassured, knowing she was not weak-willed or out of control.

With that understanding, she also learned to facilitate her decision by indulging the process, letting it work for her instead of against her. Rather than trying to avoid her uncertainty, Ellen allowed herself to think about her alternatives, and that sped up her decision. Since she also felt better about herself, it didn't take her long to decide she had to leave Joel.

THE NATURE OF ANXIETY

Anxiety is fear of the unknown. When faced with a snarling dog, you feel real fear. When faced with uncertainty, insecurity, and/or instability, you feel anxiety because you're unsure where the threat is coming from. If you feel anxious at home, it may be because you are not secure in the relationship with your partner, you lack confidence, or you are uncertain about the future together.

Understanding anxiety gives you a sense of control over it, and that, in turn, lessens the anxiety. Many studies have shown that patients who can control their own medication for pain—with a morphine pump, for example—experience less anxiety and less pain. Similarly, people who were allowed to control when they received a two-second electric shock showed less anxiety than those who had no control. Although some people prefer that a therapist assume the regulation of controlling their anxieties—through medication or providing insights—gradually taking control yourself is an important step in your growth.

The human body still responds to fear or anxiety as if it were facing an angry animal. The mind reacts to a threat to psychological safety as if it were dealing with a physical assault. Knowing what those responses are and understanding why they happen will help you keep them under control.

What follows is a description of the physiological changes in the body triggered when the mind experiences fear or anxiety. Once you know what to expect, you will be less frightened.

AROUSAL RESPONSE

1. The adrenal gland increases the adrenaline in the bloodstream. This activates the heart and muscles. The heart rate increases, and muscles become tense.
2. Respiration rate increases. The increased supply of oxygen and metabolism facilitate movement. During fear, you begin breathing heavily and your chest heaves. Under normal conditions, you breathe through muscles in the abdomen, not the chest.
3. Muscles tighten, especially in your back and nape of your neck. This protects against an attack from the rear. The muscles above the eyes also tighten, which helps you see better.
4. You may feel nauseated. The throat dries, and salivation is reduced. The colon and bladder are stimulated to expel waste products.
5. The peripheral and secondary blood vessels constrict, which directs more blood to the large muscles and the lungs.
6. Fight or flight or freeze. The body now is ready to fight or flee from the threat. But if the cause is anxiety without an obvious attacker, neither response is appropriate. Faced with a physical threat, a truly fearful situation, a person is so consumed by fighting or fleeing that he is unaware of the physical reactions.

When the responses are caused by anxiety, most people are conscious of the physical changes. They know they are panting, their heartbeat has increased, their mouth is dry, and their palms are wet. Because the changes are unpleasant and seemingly uncontrollable, many people become even more anxious, increasing the level of these responses.

As a result, if you are in a situation where you want to be in control—for example, going out with someone new—the feeling of anxiety and the responses it generates can snowball. You feel trapped, which triggers more anxiety and more reaction. If you don't learn to control your reactions or reduce your anxiety, you can become sensitized to the situations that cause them—new dates, speaking before groups, even getting on an elevator or walking into a crowded room—making your life more difficult.

Carolyn

Carolyn was upset because her lover refused to make a commitment to leave his wife. After several weeks, she called and made arrangements to meet him at a local restaurant. When she arrived, he acted coolly toward her. Sensing his rejection, Carolyn became anxious. She felt her heart throb and her mouth became dry, and she worried that she would be unable to eat.

She wanted to stay and talk about their situation, although her body seemed to be working against her. Feeling at odds with herself, Carolyn tried to get through the meal, but her throat had tightened. She couldn't swallow. She felt sick, sure that something was dreadfully wrong and wondered if she was experiencing the first signs of a heart attack.

Pretending that nothing was wrong, she continued to talk to her lover while closely monitoring her physical signs. Her fears of real illness escalated the symptoms, and she began to feel trapped.

Sitting in her seat became unbearable, but Carolyn couldn't think of a reason to leave when they were discussing something so important to both of them. As her fears built, her responses accelerated as well. Her heart beat even faster, her throat tightened more, and she began panting. Her desire to stay in the restaurant and her body's need to flee were in conflict, and she soon realized she had to get up. Her body ached from the tension in her muscles, and she began to feel faint.

Finally, Carolyn told her lover she didn't feel well and that she had to go to a hospital. Embarrassed by her reactions and angry with herself for not being able to confront her lover, she began to cry, which made her feel even worse. At the hospital, the treating physician realized she was having an anxiety attack and gave her a prescription for a tranquilizer, which turned off the arousal response.

A bright, capable woman who had developed and managed a successful industrial diamond-cutting business with her husband, Carolyn normally felt confident and had high self-esteem. After the anxiety attack, she began to doubt herself. She felt vulnerable and feared a repeat. It was as if she had a time bomb inside her, ready to go off at any time. Whenever she thought about it, she experienced the same things she felt in the restaurant and took another tranquilizer.

For the first time, Carolyn noticed a curious pattern. If she thought about her attack or what may have brought it on, she began to feel the symptoms of another attack. When she distracted herself with work, housecleaning, or talking to friends, she felt fine. In the past, she had always been able to deal directly with problems, focusing her attention and finding a solution. Now she couldn't even think about her situation.

The only way she could prevent another attack was not to think about it at all. When she began therapy, one of her first questions to me was, "How can I go about dealing with something if I can't think about it?"

Many people who suffer from anxiety attacks refuse therapy because they are afraid to think about their fears. When they do, they may experience another attack, so the easiest thing is to avoid thinking about them. It is also common to experience an attack when you can least afford one. When you most fear having an attack, your fears set your body's defensive processes in motion. In other words, you become anxious about having an anxiety attack, and that brings it on.

A major turning point in your life, such as breaking up a relationship, can easily raise your anxiety level and bring on an attack. You know exactly what you want to say to someone but feel as if your body has gone berserk when you try. Frightened by the intensity of the physical response, you try to regain control by avoiding the topic. You may try flanking maneuvers—acting obnoxiously to force a partner to leave—but refuse to think about what you are doing or the added difficulties.

Tina and Barry

Tina was the chief financial officer at a medium-sized company and regularly dealt with business crises without difficulty. But when she wanted to tell her married lover that their affair was over, she couldn't even start without feeling ill. When she was with him, she felt as if her body forced her to act like a dependent wimp.

When they dined out, Barry joked with waitresses and tried to guess which other couples were having affairs. He ignored Tina, and she felt humiliated but was unable to express her dislike of his behavior. She knew his antics were his way of dodging any serious discussion, and she was afraid that anything she said would trigger an argument and then an anxiety attack.

If neither fight nor flight is an appropriate response, the only alternative is freezing. Not acting when faced with a threat tells the mind that the situation is hopeless, the attacker is too powerful to fight and impossible to evade. The mind takes action to protect the body, shunting the blood supply from the limbs and the head to the abdomen. This is a defensive mechanism to reduce blood loss in case of injury. Often someone experiencing intense anxiety curls into a fetal position with arms and legs drawn up to protect the vital organs in the abdomen.

As a result, when the mind perceives a threat and there is no behavioral response, the mind interprets the lack of movement as freezing. The layout of the nervous system creates feedback loops that intensify the anxiety reaction, and the process snowballs, adding to the sense of danger.

CONTROLLING THE ANXIETY RESPONSE

1. Identify

The first step in overcoming anxiety and halting the symptoms is identifying your emotional response. Many people, like Carolyn, interpret anxiety attacks as the first stage of a heart attack or believe they are going insane. This naturally intensifies the attack. It is important to realize that the physical reactions are normal and designed to enhance your survival. Recognizing that the frightening symptoms are not harmful, but a natural response to your emotional state, is the first step in gaining control.

2. Breathe

Most of the systems activated by anxiety are not voluntary—we can't control heartbeat, nausea, or salivation, for example. But we can control our breathing.

The physical responses to anxiety burn up energy and require a lot of oxygen. When you become anxious, your breathing speeds up to get more oxygen into the bloodstream. When you are calm, breathing is slow, controlled by the diaphragm. But faced with a threat, the chest muscles take control, and in the effort to get more air, you may hyperventilate. When people feel anxious, they often complain about stuffiness and go outside for "air."

Deliberately slowing your breathing and reducing your

oxygen intake can curb the arousal process and help to calm you. This is why many Eastern religions use breathing exercises. Yoga, for example, emphasizes taking long, deep breaths as a method of relaxation and control.

3. Relax

The muscles over your eyebrows, known as the frontalis muscles, are particularly sensitive to stress. They tense when you feel threatened to ensure you are alert and aware of your surroundings. When they are relaxed again, the brain understands that you are no longer in danger, and the rest of the body also relaxes.

Also susceptible to stress are the trapezius, the large powerful muscles above your shoulders. They tighten to protect your neck and spinal column.

These are the main muscle groups to be aware of when you are trying to relax. Tighten them deliberately for thirty seconds, then let go. Do that several times, so you can recognize when they are relaxed and when they are tense. If necessary, rub the muscles.

Relaxing your muscles sends a strong signal to the brain that the danger is over. So does slow, deep breathing. It can also help to repeat a safety signal, such as "Everything is going to be okay." Although it may seem silly to talk to yourself, it does help, if only to prevent yourself from thinking about the potential threat.

4. Exercise

Almost any form of movement eases the muscular tension and signals the brain that you are out of danger. Moving uses the excess energy generated by anxiety, which calms you further. (However, too vigorous exercise can backfire. When you reproduce the high heart rate and rapid breathing of an anxiety attack, you may interpret them as real anxiety.)

Begin with slow, simple movements, such as walking. Gradually intensify the workout. If you can progress to a vigorous workout without triggering an anxiety response, this can be very helpful, not only for relieving the energy buildup and helping you become calm but also in strengthening the association between the arousal response and the pleasurable effects of exercise instead of anxiety.

Exercise also helps signal the brain that you are out of danger. When you are anxious, you may feel constricted, afraid to move, even of allowing your attention to wander. Another survival tactic, this focuses your concentration on your fears and the body's reluctance to move without assessing the threat. By becoming active, you send out a strong signal that you are not in danger.

5. Clench Your Fists

Endogenous opioids are naturally occurring chemicals produced by the brain when the body is injured. They can be more powerful than morphine. If you've ever been under extreme stress—in a car accident, for example, or escaping from a fire—you may have noticed that you didn't feel any pain at the time.

Tightly clenching your fists when you are having an anxiety reaction can release these opioids and help calm you.

6. Get Angry

The natural response to fear and anxiety is fight or flight. If you decide to fight, you may feel a momentary surge of fear, which you then lose sight of as you become focused on your task. Not only do your fears decrease as you confront them, you develop a more positive self-image and confidence. If you flee, you experience a momentary drop in fear as you first move away from the threat. But the relief is short-lived, quickly followed by the realization that you were unable to handle the threat or control your feelings. As a result, you develop a sense of helplessness, which in turn heightens your sensitivity to those threats.

A relatively simple technique to help you confront your

fears is to get angry at the source of the threats. Anger spurs an attack mentality and is often triggered by a sense of injustice—say, by an uncaring, unsympathetic partner. Focusing on how you are treated unfairly arouses your anger and encourages you to be more confrontational.

Gina

Gina suspected that her husband was having an affair, but she feared confronting him about it. She wasn't certain how he'd react if she asked him about it, and she had no means of supporting herself or her newborn son. Knowing this, her husband took advantage of her dependence and treated her with a disdain that increased her fears. It wasn't until he showed the same attitude toward the baby—he refused to pick him up when he was crying and looked disgusted at his weakness—that she became angry enough to confront him about his insensitivity. Having taken the plunge, she then raised the issue of his affair as well as her fear and dependence on him. For the first time in years, she felt a great sense of relief and confidence. Her renewed sense of self-worth helped save the marriage.

Now that you have some understanding of how and what an anxiety attack is, the next chapter provides additional techniques for reducing your fears and alleviating the tensions that may be produced when you consider your future.

♣ 7

Imagery

Rehearsing to Reduce Anxiety

𝒫REHISTORIC CAVE PAINTINGS ARE THOUGHT BY SOME anthropologists to represent a form of magic. Early man sketched his intended prey slain with weapons, then went off on a hunt believing he would replicate the picture. Modern psychology uses a similar technique, employing mental sketches called imagery.

Somehow, those early humans discovered the power of the imagination. It was a natural outgrowth of their most important asset: brainpower, humankind's insatiable curiosity about the rest of the world. They made and used tools, and they studied the behavior of prey animals. Thinking out a plan of attack led naturally to consideration of the expected outcome. Over time, prehistoric people recognized that the more time spent planning, the surer the results.

The modern technique of imagery developed when medical professionals realized that the brain uses the same neuropathways to process information and emotions whether they are real or imagined. That is why, for example, adults will cry recalling the pet that died in their childhood. Or why a nightmare can bring us awake, covered with perspiration and shaking with terror. Or why, if you start to think about telling your lover you want to end a relationship, you become anxious, tongue-tied, and nervous.

One study of imagery used college basketball players divided into three groups. One-third practiced foul shots for real. A second group used imagery to practice. The third group got no practice at all. The results showed that those who practiced had the greatest improvement and those with no practice had the least. But the middle group, those who only used imagery, made almost as much improvement as those who actually threw the ball.

Gymnasts, skaters, track stars, and others picture themselves doing a perfect routine, then try to duplicate that image when they go out to perform. Public speakers often use imagery to reduce pre-speech jitters.

Many therapy groups use role-playing, a form of imagery, to lessen anxiety. If someone is going on a job interview, the group may preview the situation with one person playing the interviewer while the job seeker tries different approaches for effect. Actors and musicians have long used imagery and practice to perfect their skills.

Imagery is a form of reverse conditioning. Just as Pavlov conditioned dogs to salivate when he rang a bell, you can teach yourself to respond without anxiety when you are in a difficult situation. Instead of evoking an arousal response, you condition yourself to remain calm and unemotional when faced with a situation that formerly upset you.

Slowing your breathing and using relaxation techniques to control the physical reactions of the arousal response is a bit like taking a tranquilizer. These strategies temporarily help you feel better and gain confidence, but they don't eliminate the cause of the anxiety. What is needed is a psychological strategy to overcome the unknown fear that is provoking the fearful reaction.

Since there are as many causes of anxiety as there are people, most of those responses are learned. Our experience has taught us that something—a spider, a drunk spouse, being alone—poses a threat. When we come across the same conditions we grow alert and prepared. If we learn that our anxiety outweighs the potential threat, we can reduce both the threat and our fear of it. Learned behavior can eventually be unlearned; we just need a new set of conditioning.

When a relationship is ending, it may be necessary to

recondition two kinds of responses. For example, a woman may need to face her fears of living alone or finding new friends. But she must also reduce her own positive responses to the ex's looks, or cooking skills, or sense of humor. She has to desensitize both her anxieties and her feelings of attraction.

Rewards—feeling good, being loved, feeling secure—are the conditioning in a relationship. When you love someone, you become attached emotionally and intellectually. The intellectual attachment is based on whether the person meets your needs: Is he the type of person you are looking for? Does she have good character and values? Does he treat you well?

The emotional attachment comes from how the person makes you feel. In effect, the emotional link is determined by how involuntary organs—heart, stomach, nerve centers, lungs—are conditioned by your lover.

As you spend time together, you explore and develop mutual needs and considerations. You also become conditioned in a positive way to each other. The happiness and pleasure you feel become associated with your lover. Being with him or her makes you feel good, and that strengthens the emotional bond between you. After a while, just the thought or sight of your lover brings a smile, a feeling of elation, a sense of security—all strong positive associations.

When the relationship is over, it may be as difficult for you to break that conditioning as it was for old firehorses to stop reacting to the sound of an alarm. This chapter teaches you how to desensitize yourself, how to change the conditioning and responses that developed with your lover.

AVOIDANCE VS. EXPOSURE

The first step is gradually to allow yourself to experience the negative feelings even though they make you feel bad. You use imagery techniques at first until you feel confident about coping with them in reality. If you try to avoid fears, you only perpetuate their anxiety-evoking effect.

For example, if you're afraid of elevators and always take the stairs, you'll never get over your fear of elevators. But if you make yourself take an elevator for one floor, then two, then three, etc., you will eventually overcome the dread. Numerous studies and experiments have proven that avoidance perpetuates fears whereas repeated exposure extinguishes them.

Similarly, if you refuse to allow yourself to experience your apprehension about confronting your lover, that fear will continue to have power over you. The only way to regain control is to face up to fears, even if it also means thinking about the associated anxieties over finances, children, and loneliness. You have to allow yourself to experience those feelings in order to get rid of them. If you dread telling your lover you want to end the relationship but avoid thinking about it because you become so anxious and upset, those negative feelings will persist, making it even more difficult for you to act.

IMAGERY VS. REALITY

To begin with, fears confronted using imagery are less intense than when faced in reality. Telling your lover you've had it and walking out the door is much more stressful than visualizing those actions. For many people, the intensity of the emotions that arise when they only consider ending a relationship are so strong that they are reluctant to think about it, let alone take action. What is needed is a way to reduce the intensity, and that's where imagery is valuable.

By repeatedly considering the various scenarios in this kind of confrontation, you gradually reduce your apprehension. Over time, you can imagine the scene and appraise all of your possible responses to your partner's probable reaction. This gives you a sense of control and reduces your stress level. When you decide to turn your imagery into reality—and you can make the choice when you feel comfortable—you will feel less anxious and uptight about it.

Since the mind uses the same pathways to process imagery as it does reality, practice makes you familiar with the feelings evoked and gives you control over your emotional reactions. If, for example, you are facing a range of situations that make you anxious and tense, you can use imagery to rehearse your responses over a period of time at the rate you find adequate. You practice when you are comfortable and at leisure, stopping when you get too upset, then returning when you feel relaxed again. With imagery, you can regulate the intensity of the feelings and reactions, their duration, and when you evoke them.

Self-directed imagery, therefore, allows you to focus on the material when it is convenient for you. It gives you control over your exposure to the situation to suit your needs—frequent, long practice yields faster control; short, infrequent exposure means slower extinction of those stressful reactions. You can also select the order in which you evoke the emotional responses and bring them under control.

Further, you can choose the scene—which means you can be sure it is relevant to your anxieties—and maintain your focus on it for a longer period than normal. You can speed up your command of the negative feelings that scene evokes by increasing the number of times you decide to experience it. This is often more effective than allowing the mind to choose its own time and scene to ponder.

Many people like to take long walks when they use imagery. While walking, the mind can focus on whatever it considers a top priority. When these images arise, it is easier to concentrate on them if you are also engaged in an activity that provides some pleasure and a natural release of energy. If the images become too painful or intense, you can distract yourself by looking at scenery or passersby.

Eventually, of course, you have to face your fears in reality.

If you decide to tell your lover that you no longer love him, you open yourself up to potential problems. You can't be sure of his reaction—he may get angry, offer arguments to counter your reasons, or raise issues that undermine your position. If you have used imagery to rehearse the scene, you probably have considered some or all of his options and developed your own responses to them. You have reduced the intensity of your feelings, enabling you to confront him with restraint and poise.

Carolyn, described in the previous chapter, rehearsed her next confrontation with her lover for several weeks. When she felt she had lowered her anxiety level, she set up a meeting and told him she wanted to end the affair. He became very upset and begged her for more time. He played on her guilt feelings, arguing it was not fair to give an ultimatum to someone you loved. He raved about reporting her to her boss. But Carolyn was prepared for his tactics and calmly held her position. Eventually, her composure prevailed and they were able to discuss the situation more constructively.

Real-life confrontations have some advantages. It is difficult to imagine some situations without experiencing them. Exposure in reality desensitizes some issues faster. You are faced with the full array of possibilities, more than you could imagine, and you have to face them. This "dive in the deep end" approach is effective with mild fears; its effectiveness with more intense anxieties is typically balanced by the determination to avoid any similar confrontations.

Bad planning, bad timing, and unpredictable responses can discourage you from trying the approach again. Abrupt reality may lead to faster desensitization, but the lack of control over uncomfortable feelings encourages most people to find pleasanter ways of facing problems. Gradual exposure to anxieties and rehearsal through imagery provides confidence-building experiences that lead to continued practice and practical application.

USING IMAGERY TO BREAK BONDS

If your partner is extremely jealous, for example, and you are fed up with his accusations and control, you may still be reluctant to leave because you are afraid of being on your own. You fear the solitude and worry about supporting yourself. Whenever you contemplate breaking up with him, those fears are your first consideration, making you so anxious and tense you can't take action despite your unhappiness.

Imagery can be particularly helpful in reducing the stress in that situation and providing the necessary tools to make an appropriate decision.

First of all, it is important to understand that emotional bonds to someone are not sacred. They can be manipulated in the same way other feelings are. (I discuss this in greater detail in Chapter Nine.) People form emotional attachments to the wrong partner all the time. If you love someone who has become an alcoholic or drug abuser, there is no reason to remain in that relationship. But most people have little experience taking an active role in altering their feelings toward someone, so they remain trapped in dangerous situations.

Emotional reactions, like most others, are based on association. For example, you can't blush on command. But if you are asked to blush and can recall an embarrassing situation, you will blush. In the same way, actors who have to cry remember a sad experience from childhood, and the tears flow. And people often use sexual fantasies to put themselves in the mood when a partner wants intercourse.

Many feelings are triggered by past associations in your life. If you were mugged in the office parking lot, you will be fearful every time you have to go to your car. If you nearly drowned in a heavy surf, swimming in the ocean will be difficult and stressful. If you use imagery to conjure up a picture of rough seas while at home, imagining yourself swimming strongly to shore, you can reduce your anxiety because the image becomes associated with safety and competence, not danger and weakness.

Most of us have a long string of fears, anxieties, and phobias of greater or lesser importance. In order to use imagery effectively, it is helpful to organize those issues that cause the most intense feelings by constructing a hierarchy.

Begin by finding a peaceful spot to be alone. Get some paper and a pen. Allow yourself to think about your problems without direction. Which issues cause the most intense reaction? Note the situations that make you the most fearful, anxious, or insecure. If possible, arrange your fears within each issue from least to most intense—for example, under separating, you might include: confrontation, independence, finances, safety, boredom.

Now you can start with the least intense fear of the least intense situation, say, using public transportation to get to a new job. Use the imagery techniques to face each of your anxieties: planning a route, getting the schedule, timing a commute, waiting for a bus. As you get comfortable with the alternatives for each, move on to the next one. If something is disturbing, stop and start at the beginning again until you feel more confident.

Let's assume that you're afraid of living on your own. Whenever you think about leaving your partner and going off by yourself, you become nervous and tense. There could be countless reasons why you feel that way—perhaps you lost a number of jobs before your marriage and associate being single with rejection and frustration. What is important now is to end the association your mind makes between living alone and feeling anxious.

The first step is to imagine yourself being independent. You will feel the negative emotions you usually do, but you're in a safe situation. Allow yourself to experience those emotions for a few minutes. Then stop and do something else. After a period of time, again bring up the image of living alone and experience the emotions for another few minutes. After repeatedly visualizing this image in a safe setting, the negative emotions abate and the image becomes associated with safety.

Again, knowing why something triggers an emotional response usually doesn't have much effect on reducing the intensity of that response. For example, knowing that you fear cars because you were in an accident doesn't lessen your fear. Regardless of the circumstances that led to the initial association, the important thing now is to establish a new pattern. You have to teach yourself to connect independence with safety.

Once you have reduced the initial fears, slowly think about the reasons for your anxiety. Although they are not critical in the first step of changing your association, it is helpful to face them directly. Avoiding fearful situations helps to increase the reaction because there's no information to counter it. Confronting fears, even in your mind, eases the anxiety level. Imagery gives you time, distance, and control so you can look at alternatives, consider consequences, and develop choices.

There may be practical reasons, such as lack of job skills, that are involved in your fear of independence. It is sensible to be concerned about living alone if you don't have a way of supporting yourself, but that is a problem you can correct. A training program or school can supply the skills you need.

Intellectually based fears are best undone with practical, logical solutions. Emotionally based fears are controlled with imagery. Typically, we have more difficulty overcoming the emotional fears. Once those are eliminated, most of us work on reducing the intellectual fears by finding day care, taking a course, and so on.

Overcoming emotionally based fears is not easy. The process, even using imagery, can be painful. When you conjure up a picture of being independent, for example, you trigger your anxieties. This can cause hyperventilation, rapid heartbeat, and nausea. That is why you should use imagery sparingly at first, starting slowly with the less intense anxieties and gradually extending the frequency and duration.

Begin with the least fearful images and practice at a time and in a place where you feel safe and secure. If you fear solitude, imagine yourself living alone but near family or friends. Picture yourself entertaining coworkers or chatting with neighbors at the pool. Think about enjoying a home-cooked meal while watching your favorite movie without a distraction or argument. Play with the image for a few minutes, then let it go.

Don't stay with an image or scene if it becomes too uncomfortable. Stop, go back to the beginning, and go over the easier steps—perhaps furnishing a new apartment—and try a new approach for the difficult part. Take each forward movement only as far as it feels comfortable, part of a flow or current.

The main requirement to overcoming emotional triggers is a willingness to tolerate some discomfort at levels you set for yourself. And even that discomfort can be minimized. Remember, the mind places the highest priority on survival issues. Breaking off a relationship and starting your life in new circumstances usually takes precedence over most other problems and focuses your attention. Even at work, if you are not actively concentrating on a task at hand, your mind wanders to the problems in your personal life.

Often this is so painful and distracting that you refocus and concentrate on your current task and circumstance. As a result, even thinking about your personal situation becomes associated with anxiety and tenseness. The way to regain control is to allow yourself to consider your situation whenever it comes into your head. Think it through for a few minutes, then go back to what you were doing.

Promise yourself you will set aside specific time to think about it again when you leave work. Find your safe setting and a few minutes of free time and give yourself permission to reflect. Let your mind poke and probe and ponder whatever takes precedence. Try to back off mentally and just allow your mind to consider whatever pops up. Then allow yourself to consider it and think it through.

If you can put yourself in the role of bystander, you will notice that you go through a number of scenarios, testing each one. This is an examination process, probing the potential consequences for various alternatives—an unannounced confrontation, a slow buildup, an ultimatum, pointed arguments. Each choice has strengths and weaknesses: The confrontation could make him angry; you may not be able to keep an ultimatum right now; you may need time to acquire job skills. This process allows you to explore them all.

Obviously, some of the alternatives are going to be painful, and all will probably be anxiety provoking. But you are scouting them mentally, not committing yourself, and the mind is desensitizing itself as each alternative is considered. Over time, you will not feel as intensely about them and can then make a decision without those emotional bonds. The ambivalence and hesitation also ensure that all sides will be fully considered and weighed.

Because the mind uses the same pathways to process both reality and imagination, your physical responses will be activated. If you are afraid of living alone and imagine life by yourself, you will feel nervous and uncomfortable at first. Allow yourself to slowly consider your negative attitude and why you feel that way. Try to find solutions to your concerns. If you're worried about loneliness, add images of friends, family, coworkers, neighbors. If finances concern you, include plans to take courses, network for a new job, or take some other specific action.

The physical symptoms of the arousal response described earlier may occur. Remember to take long, deep breaths to slow your breathing and heartbeat. Walking or any kind of movement helps alleviate tension by stretching taut muscles. Even if you can't get up and walk around, just flexing your muscles, then relaxing them, helps. Massaging the forehead and the nape of neck also eases tightness and reduces anxiety.

Knowing you have that control is reassurance that you are

not having a heart attack or going insane. Ambivalence, uncertainty, and hesitation are all strategies for reducing the potential for bad decisions. Ignoring the mind's natural instinct to probe any hazard and to examine every escape route is ultimately more stressful than experiencing the discomfort and anxiety engendered by trying to control access to priority concerns. Allowing free rein gives you time to conjure up positive images to counter your fears, instead of hiding them away and adding to them.

Your mind is instinctively protective. If the material is very disturbing, the focus changes quickly and distractions are embraced willingly. Periodically, the stressful thoughts resurface then sink again, each time floating for progressively longer periods until they linger enough to be considered. In the same manner, you gradually enure yourself to a bath full of very hot water.

Control is important, but forcing your mind to consider unpleasant areas too soon or for too long can work against the process. Even the most negative aspects of your problems will be explored eventually, as you become desensitized to them. If some issues don't raise too many disturbing reactions, you may choose to prolong your exposure. That speeds up the desensitization and brings you relief that much sooner. Keep in mind that if you push yourself too hard, you may make the experience so unpleasant and uncomfortable that you abandon it.

There is a tendency to be in a hurry to get to the end step—bidding your ex good-bye, packing your car, and driving off. But this may be too discouraging at first. Work on getting yourself strong and over your fears. Taking small bits, you'll be amazed how far you go. Each step should be a small, smooth, gentle move from the one before. Go slowly and easily.

Many people are reluctant to use the imagery process because they don't want to have negative thoughts, even about a dying relationship. But ambivalence, anxiety, and uncertainty are normal and healthy feelings that promote survival. Indeed, it is unhealthy to maintain a positive attitude about a negative situation. Denying strong emotions because they bring negative thoughts and feelings is counterproductive. These emotions will well up somehow, usually at an inopportune moment.

Advocates of positive thinking emphasize an optimistic, upbeat outlook: Happy thoughts are the key to health, success, and joy. Carried to extremes, this philosophy ignores the natural role of worry, especially in the face of real threats. If you don't allow yourself to worry or entertain negative scenarios, you will neither learn from your mistakes nor plan for dangerous situations. It is difficult to consider survival techniques if you don't even recognize the potential threat.

Used sparingly, positive thinking can help you test new possibilities. For example, if you are suddenly on your own, thinking positively about yourself will motivate you to meet new people. It can also help you maintain hope, a happy attitude, and a sense of humor, all aids in overcoming problems. But trying to sustain giddiness in the face of disaster is irrational. Positive thinking without objective analysis is not a substitute for the mind's natural tendency to set priorities on survival-oriented issues, problems, and threatening possibilities.

Positive thinking can be another strategy to avoid thinking about or acting on a problem. Some people use denial, refusing to recognize any rough spot. Others rationalize, explaining how uncontrollable circumstances such as illness, bankruptcy, or handicaps make it impossible for them to consider leaving an abusive spouse.

Other avoidance strategies are procrastination and even therapy. Professional help can be useful, but not if it is a tactic to postpone an inevitable confrontation and separation. Some people get so involved with work, hobbies, and sports that they have no time for problems at home. Others become depressed, unable to do anything about anything. Social withdrawal, emotional numbness, or self-destructive behavior may be symptoms of avoidance.

It is enticing just to escape your problems, especially when you don't feel any progress toward their solution. You may have practiced imagery for a few weeks, considering the possibility of leaving your partner. You are so worried about being independent, being alone, paying all your own expenses, and feeling isolated from other people that you are beginning to feel obsessive. It seems as if you can't get past the panic and anxiety that develop whenever you try to think about your future.

Movement and progress come in fits and starts because the priorities change as each aspect of your life is considered. As your mind focuses on each area, that subject gradually becomes desensitized. As one anxiety abates, the mind moves on to consider the new high priority. For example, if you fear being alone, then realize you will be near friends and family, loneliness becomes less sensitive. Then you start worrying about money because that now has a higher priority and therefore a higher anxiety level.

Because of the pattern of lowering fear A on your anxiety scale and then moving to fear B, which now is higher, it is difficult to recognize progress as long as your overall anxiety level remains high. The intensity won't diminish until the mind has reduced *all* the subissues. Then you feel plateaued at that stage until each subissue has been further reduced.

To complicate the process, desensitization is not linear. Progress is usually two steps forward and one step back. Boats rigged with triangular sails are able to move against the wind if they take a zigzag course, known as tacking. Similarly, you will make headway against your fears if you recognize that a sideways motion can also be progress. Once you've reduced fear A to six and concentrate on the other fears, A may lose some ground. If it takes several weeks to bring the other issues down from level eight, fear A may even move up to seven.

This discourages people who want a straight line and no backsliding.

Reconditioning is a slow, uncomfortable process that causes some emotional pain. It must be worked at and taken seriously if it is to be successful. Each time you bring up the problem and your worries, you scrape away some of the barnacles of your fears and increase your control over your direction. The changes are incremental, but they are real.

The rebounding is called spontaneous recovery and works for both positive and negative emotions. For example, suppose that you listen to a new song so many times that it no longer appeals to you. Five years later you hear it again, and you still like it, but not as much as originally. Most pleasures wear out their welcome if overexposed. After a respite, they usually regain their attraction, but at a lesser intensity.

Spontaneous recovery helps to explain the lack of apparent forward progress. One possible explanation for spontaneous recovery is that repeated exposure to a fearful image desensitizes fear in two distinct ways. The first, as I discussed, is that the image—say, of being alone—gradually becomes associated with safety rather than fear. The second is that by repeatedly reactivating the fearful image, the emotional response is temporarily fatigued. With rest, the component due to fatigue rebounds, giving the false impression that the fears have regained their strength on their own. As I've emphasized, desensitization is a slow process that requires time, effort, and patience. It takes willpower and understanding to expose yourself repeatedly to thinking that is uncomfortable and stressful, but eventually the exertion pays dividends.

Once the emotional reactions have lost their association with anxiety and uncertainty, the underlying issue is typically easy to resolve. Without the baggage of negative feelings, you can logically weigh the pros and cons and come to a resolution of your problems. You can apply these new skills whenever emotional issues threaten your happiness, security, or safety.

‣ 8

The Bonds of Love

HOUDINI MANAGED HIS ESCAPES BY KNOWING PRE-cisely how his restraints worked. To break out of a destructive relationship, it is necessary to understand how love binds two people. Or to give another analogy, if you want to take something apart, it helps to know how it was put together in the first place. That is true of a car, a house, or a relationship.

If you understand what attracts you to the main person in your life, if you can identify the threads that make up the fabric of your relationship, you can begin to unravel it. These are different in every pairing because we each bring our own unique history and experiences, but the general outlines are relevant to everyone.

Love, like other emotions, has three basic components: behavioral, psychological, and emotional. Each of these, in turn, may be expressed in any number of ways. What follows are examples of some of the most common ways these components are put together between two people. They may seem obvious, but identifying and defining even the most ordinary actions increases understanding, and that's the first step in cutting yourself loose.

BEHAVIORAL BONDS—ACTS OF LOVE

Behavioral bonds begin with the most obvious: making love with each other, expressing concern and care for each other, saying "I love you." They also include touching, hugging, cuddling, and other physical expressions of one's feelings. Other behavioral expressions part of everyday life are sharing activities, chores, and responsibilities.

Two people who spend a lot of time together but have no passion or sense of commitment have behavioral bonds only. They lack the emotional (passion) and psychological (mutual exclusivity or trust).

Murleen and Andrew had been married for seven years when they realized their relationship had deteriorated. The strain of two children when they were barely out of their teens turned them against each other. Andrew worked two jobs and tried to be involved with the children but felt his efforts weren't appreciated. He resented Murleen's lack of support and distanced himself.

She, in turn, resented his lack of care and concern, so she became more negative and even less supportive. This vicious spiral pushed them farther and farther apart.

By the time they came in for counseling, the marriage was little more than shared chores and responsibilities. They shopped together, went out to eat or to a movie, but neither felt any commitment, care, or trust for the other. They were no longer sexually intimate and rarely spoke about anything beyond the immediate needs of home and children. They were talking about a divorce. After some counseling, they were able to understand each other's position better and reestablished their relationship.

Maggie and Joe had both been married before. After they married, they started a trucking business, which consumed their time. Joe was happy with this arrangement, but after five years, Maggie was dissatisfied. Their lives were tied to the business and doing household chores. There was no joy in their marriage, and she was just going through the motions.

Joe insisted that he still loved her, but Maggie was less sure of her feelings. She considered him a practical part of her life, necessary for financial support and companionship. She tried to work on their problems but finally decided he didn't want to change. He always put the business first, and Maggie felt she was way down on his list.

She decided to work less in the trucking business and took a part-time job as a cocktail waitress. Once she was financially secure, she moved out. About a year later, she met someone who was not a workaholic. They eventually married and had a relationship more fulfilling than the one she had with Joe.

Behavioral bonds are relatively easy to break. One or both partners need only find something more appealing. If two people merely share chores and activities, both can gain by finding someone with whom they can also experience passion, trust, and commitment—the full range of emotions meant by love.

PSYCHOLOGICAL BONDS

These are the feelings most people primarily associate with love. They include caring, companionship, trust, friendship, loyalty, commitment, mutual understanding, support, shared attitudes and values, fulfillment of needs, shared interests and activities, and the need for approval and affiliation.

In a relationship based on psychological bonds, one partner may feel that he or she has found the perfect mate, but the other may not be satisfied. Other signs of a problem are a lack of shared activities and passion. This situation is often found in couples who stay together for fear of the effects of a divorce on their children. Or people may remain together for religious or financial reasons long after their relationship has died.

Neal is a narcissist who manipulated Carol and his family to meet his needs. He was intelligent and personable and he used those qualities to get his way all the time. He made all the decisions in their marriage: what they bought, who their friends were, where and when they vacationed. He used persuasion, not coercion, but everything was done the way he wanted it.

Carol thought he was entitled to the special consideration because he was a genius and beyond the rules for ordinary people. He couldn't be expected to act like everyone else. She defended his freewheeling approach and overlooked his flagrant lapses in behavior. With the help of counseling, Carol eventually realized that Neal was an abuser who manipulated her into dependency and didn't deserve her loyalty and trust. She also learned that he had been having affairs throughout their marriage. Once she understood how self-absorbed Neal was, she was able to leave him and get on with her life.

Martha admired and respected Luke's dedication to his work and family, but he always seemed to be on the verge of anger. He never saw the bright side in anything. Rigid and depressed, he seemed to be waiting for something terrible to happen, always looking for potential problems. Martha loved him, trusted him, and was committed to him, but he wasn't any fun to be around. She thought Luke's attitude was destroying her and the family and begged him to go for help. When he refused, she decided to leave, knowing he couldn't change without it.

Ellie and Phil were both in their fifties. He was very knowledgeable and loved to teach. Ellie was an eager student. When they were together, he drank continually. She married him anyway, only to see the drinking increase and the lessons diminish. He insisted he was too educated to help her with the menial chores, but he couldn't afford to hire help. She was very energetic and devoted to him, so she indulged him.

Phil liked to relax with friends, who were also drinkers. That meant lots of extra work for Ellie, but she didn't mind at first. Over time, though, she realized he was an alcoholic who cared more for his bottle than for her. He showed no real respect or concern for her needs. He indulged himself at her expense and was too far gone to change. When she threatened to leave, he promised to change, but he never did. Eventually, she got tired and moved out.

The line between abuse and care is usually thinner than we imagine. Ellie loved Phil and admired his education and knowledge. She thrived on his dependence on her to take care of him. For a long time, it made her feel secure and wanted. It was only when she realized he was an alcoholic who was using her for his own ends that the relationship became intolerable and she was able to break free.

Under the best of circumstances, a once grand romance may turn into a friendship. Each partner provides the other with some psychological needs such as companionship, loyalty, commitment, and support. But the relationship rarely fills any emotional spaces for either person.

More often, the emotional vacuum turns the relationship into an armed camp. The pair stay together for the sake of the kids or because their families don't believe in divorce or because it would hurt someone's career, but they feed off each other's needs. The marriage is seriously flawed. In some cases, it brings out the worst characteristics of both partners. In others, the couple maintains a harmonious, if passionless, arrangement.

The psychological bond is difficult to untie. One of the most effective methods requires some hard judgments and analysis. It demands honesty and clear thinking about the partner. For example, once you discover that he or she is not trustworthy, not truly interested in your well-being, or has different values and attitudes about life and love, then the psychological bond can be broken. (Chapter Thirteen provides more detail on how to recognize and escape from a relationship of psychological bonds.)

EMOTIONAL BONDS

Probably the most important emotional tie is sexual arousal. But there are other ways a relationship can arouse or calm the partners. For example, one partner may fear loneliness or rejection. Being in a relationship may lessen one partner's need to dominate and control others or reduce anxieties about disapproval from family and friends or about the future. A relationship may provide a sense of security, safety, and happiness through the pleasure and joy of being half of a pair. It can stimulate the sense of adventure and growth, provide a safe haven against outside problems, and reassure someone concerned about external dangers.

Other emotional bonds include many of the emotions associated with grief when the pair is separated. One or both members may feel anxious, hypervigilant, preoccupied with reuniting, irritable, restless, angry, or sad. They may have difficulty concentrating or sleeping or be tense. Just knowing a separation from a partner is in the future, even a temporary one, may evoke anxiety.

When Anita is between men, she is afraid to go to parties alone. She even lacks confidence in job interviews. Without a man around, she feels incomplete, like the old song, "You're nobody 'til somebody loves you." Desperate for confirmation of her sense of self, she grabs onto whatever man shows an interest in her, usually someone who is domineering and controlling. Her need to be dependent attracts men who want a clingy woman. They eventually leave because she is too demanding of their attention and presence, and she ends up alone again, looking for the next man to bring life to her existence.

Sex—an emotional bond—is the glue in some affairs. Such relationships lack the other components of love, especially commitment, loyalty, and trust. The partners rarely do anything together outside of the bedroom, focusing only on sexual gratification and fulfilling each other's fantasies.

Often the initial excitement is so great and the attraction so powerful that the urge to be with the partner can lead to poor judgment and reckless behavior. Many people throw caution to the winds—giving up a job, apartment, ties to friends or family, and other anchors—to meet the demands of an exciting new romantic partner. Within a year, as the passion and novelty fade, the relationship is over. The pair realize they have nothing in common, and the person who changed the most, usually the woman, finds herself having to rebuild some bridges.

Sean loved Nadine. She was beautiful and carefree, while his wife was caught up in her own world, caring for their two young children and her teaching job. Sean left his family and moved in with Nadine. For the first month, they had sex every night. By the end of the second month, he was back with his wife.

In counseling, he explained that the terrific sex had captivated him and he was unable to see beyond it. But after two months of steady indulgence, the pleasure faded and he realized he had nothing in common with Nadine. She was great in bed, but that was all.

Don was a workaholic. His wife, Helen, accepted it and developed her own life, centered on their children and her activities with the Girl Scouts and the school library fund. But she resented his distance and took revenge when she could. She refused to have sex with him and frequently put him down in conversations.

Realizing that Helen no longer loved him, Don considered divorce, but he was afraid of being alone. Although the marriage was a sham, being with Helen calmed his fears. He was terrified that he would never meet anyone else.

When he came in for counseling, there seemed no reason to try to work things out between them. Neither was interested in reviving their marriage. Instead, Don concentrated on overcoming his fears of being alone so he could face the divorce.

Dick's wife was a control freak and he could no longer live with her. For years, he had tried to please her, working hard, helping with the children, and taking over most of the household chores as well. Nevertheless, she always had a complaint. She told other people that "He just thinks of himself." "He's only interested in his work." "He wants everything his way." Dick realized there was no hope, but he was afraid of the unknown and couldn't make himself leave. He hung on for years, hoping she would change, trying to make the marriage work.

Once he finally made the break, Dick regretted all the years he had spent trying to make things better with someone who refused to make any effort at all. Looking back, he realized that his fear of life without his wife cost him dearly.

The emotional ties are the most difficult to break. We naturally like the things that make us happy. People indulge in activities they enjoy, until prolonged exposure eventually dulls the pleasure. Joys fade unless they are nourished. Fears thrive until they are confronted.

Interestingly, each partner may have different ties to the relationship. For example, a woman who remains with an abusive man may be psychologically or behaviorally dependent on him. He stays in the pairing because it fills his psychological or emotional need to control someone else. People look to fill their own emotional spaces in the important relationships in their lives, and they are different for each of us. In good relationships, the people involved both give and take.

In bad ones, the lack of balance produces tension and stress that affect everyone.

A relationship that begins with passion can turn into true love as the partners learn more about each other and begin to care, just as friendship may evolve into a more intimate relationship. An affair or marriage that provides only one or two of the basic components at any time is not necessarily doomed to self-destruct. That may be what one or both of those involved need at the particular moment. At another time, the balance may shift as the pair adjusts and grows and circumstances change.

Relationships, like the people in them, mutate to reflect outside forces. It is only when the two people involved show pathological needs or emotions over long periods of time that separation may be the best choice. For example, if your partner is addicted to drugs or alcohol, is abusive or unfaithful, it may be time for you to sever the ties and look for a healthier situation. Some problems are less threatening but equally corrosive. If your mate is abusive or overly narcissistic or showing symptoms of any serious personality disorder, the wisest move is probably to save yourself.

Usually, the mind recognizes the need for escape. As discussed, that need may be the source of tension, physical ailments, and emotional chaos if you fail to respond to the threat to your sense of self. As hard as it is, it is necessary to act on such dangers. Delaying only postpones the inevitable.

The next step in breaking the ties that bind you to a destructive relationship is knowing what has to be severed. As explained above, every pairing has its own pattern, just as every building has its own blueprint. Just as it is important to know what are the particular beams and supporting walls if the building is coming down, it is important to know what are the reinforcements in the relationship you are trying to demolish.

HEALTHY BONDS

A healthy, growing relationship develops between people who show traits associated with good character: trustworthiness, honesty, dependability, thoughtfulness, sincerity, caring, and sensitivity. If a lover's behavior toward you and others demands constant excuses and apologies, the potential for building a strong relationship is limited.

When two people share not only sexual intimacy, but also plans for the future, worries and concerns about life in general, problems at work, successes and failures, they develop bonds of commitment, concern, and caring. Discussing problems, offering support in bad times and cheer in good ones, investing in a partner's hopes and dreams, making financial plans, showing loyalty and faith in each other—these are all the ties that make a lifelong commitment between two people, the foundation for a marriage and family that turns a house into a home. Here are the qualities to look for in a partner and a relationship:

- Permanence and stability over time, not just the demands of here and now

- Someone who is an equal, not a fantasy-come-true who makes you feel jealous and possessive

- Slow but steady growth in intimacy, not the quick heat of infatuation

- A lover who shares some interests, not one who is an enigmatic challenge

- Someone who shares pleasures, not just shows you a good time

- Reliability and dependability, not a catastrophe junkie always dealing with emergencies, lawyers, and cops

- Balance and moderation, not obsession and ambition

- Someone who values your independence and wants to make you happy, not someone who plays on your needs and encourages your dependence

- A full and equal partner, not a sidekick or fan

Matt and Linda

A divorced elementary school teacher, Linda concentrated on her work, her two teenage sons, and her family. She socialized with close friends on the weekends, used golf and skiing to keep fit, and generally made a new life for herself.

After six years she met Matt. His own marriage had ended two years earlier, and he also had two teenage sons. Not particularly ambitious or aggressive, his job as head of the regional sales department for a pharmaceutical company kept him busy. In his spare time he enjoyed tennis, golf, bowling, and cross-country skiing, not for the competition, but just to keep his tall, thin body in shape. A sociable man with a good sense of humor, Matt liked dining out, museums, walks in the park, movies and theater, even regular visits with his parents.

They met at a tennis party when they were randomly paired as a doubles team. Matt immediately liked Linda's approach—serious and intent on playing well but also having fun and socializing. He invited her for coffee and more similarities became apparent: each ordered decaf because both had plans for early morning exercise with friends. He asked her out for dinner later in the week and she accepted. He liked her independence and her acceptance of him. She was attracted to him for many of the same reasons, particularly his recognition of her independence.

Although they realized almost immediately they would marry eventually, it was three years before they did. They both wanted to see their children in college first. During the courtship, each had time to meet and become comfortable with the other's family and friends. Since neither felt a need to dominate or control the relationship, those ties were encouraged and developed. They enjoyed each other's world as well as the one they shared. Their sex life was satisfying and comfortable, as filled with cuddling as with passion.

Together, they have a good relationship based on commitment and trust. They share friendship as well as many interests. Their partnership requires love and equality and a recognition that situations change. They interchange responsibilities in some areas while maintaining special roles as well, a balance between cooperation and assertiveness. They share with each other, and each makes the other happy.

Matt and Linda are both planners but are willing to make modifications as need arises. They decided to use extra savings for education expenses, not retirement funds as originally planned, for example. And they decided against a vacation house in favor of investing the money and using the interest to finance trips to see their children. Even when difficulties developed, they have relied on each other to survive and prosper. When Matt lost his job, he did household chores for eighteen months while Linda worked. He was back at work when Linda developed Lyme disease. For a year, she couldn't do any of the sports they enjoyed together, but Matt was there to help and support her. He's working and she feels better and their marriage continues to grow.

A relationship based on balance, independence, commitment, and trust is healthy and positive. It allows both parties to grow and stretch and does not set up restrictions, demands, absolutes, or controls. In the best of all possible worlds, both partners would always be equal, but that rarely happens. Depending on situation and circumstance, one or the other partner may be dominant for part of the time, but eventually things even out. For example, a woman may decide to stop working after the birth of a child, but in a healthy relationship, that doesn't mean she no longer has a say in how money is spent. Or a man may become ill and rely on his partner to make decisions, earn money, and provide emotional support until his recovery.

Healthy relationships are in a state of flux. When neither person needs to dominate, power and control flow between the two, depending on ability and need. It is only when one person demands authority over the other all the time that a relationship deteriorates. It is the behavior over time that indicates the strength or weakness of the ties between two people, not a frozen frame at any specific moment.

In general, healthy relationships help you feel good about yourself, your mate, and the future. You are assured of love, respect, and support no matter what happens. You enjoy the time you spend together and find pleasure when you're alone as well. If circumstances create emergencies, there is no sense of looming catastrophe. If serious problems do develop, you are confident of companionship, comfort, and love to get you through.

On the other hand, a relationship dominated by one partner's personal quirks is in trouble. Whenever one person demands control over another, the lack of balance puts both in jeopardy. Usually the dominant partner sets the boundaries and interprets the rules, changing them on a whim and keeping the other partner off-balance, unprepared, and dependent.

The next chapters provide guidelines for breaking away from relationships, regardless of the ties that bind.

✿ 9

Breaking up Is Hard to Do

Cutting Emotional Bonds

Ultimately, this book is about being a survivor, not a victim. A person may be victimized as a member of a minority group, the object of a rape or mugging, the subject of inaccurate gossip, or the partner in an abusive or impossible relationship. But a survivor comes to terms with the difficult times and creates a more promising future.

Victims blame the past for present difficulties and future insecurities. By refusing to recognize their own responsibility for their problems, victims don't learn from mistakes and don't take action to change the situation. Someone else is at fault, and that someone should make amends or at least pay for the victim's suffering and pain.

Surviving a bad relationship means cutting your losses, honestly assessing your reactions, and investing some time and effort into confronting your anxieties. A first step is examining your initial attraction to your partner. Being aware of and alert to inconsistencies, disappointments, and reality helps you objectively analyze your situation. To escape from an emotional bond means facing up to the fears and unnamed hopes that tie you two together.

GROWTH AND CHANGE

Being human, being alive, is about growth and change, adaptation and learning. Whatever restricts an individual's ability to grow and learn must be examined and evaluated. People have needs beyond the basic requirements of food and water;

they have rights as individuals independent of a relationship. Connections that depend on violence, threats, intimidation, control, restrictions, rigidity, and/or secretiveness limit the growth of both partners. Fear of change, unwillingness to compromise, nostalgia for vague and undefined "old days"— these are all signs of a need for control and rigidity that limits a relationship and endangers the mental balance of those involved.

Moving beyond a relationship tied by emotional bonds takes strength, honesty, courage, support, and effort. These ties are the most difficult to break and require the unhappy partner to face up to fears as well as problems. Often one or both people in any long-standing relationship are soothing an emotional itch no matter how impossible it seems to outsiders. The apparent imbalance in a marriage may be adjustments for the needs or desires of those involved. Leaving that arrangement behind can be very disturbing and uncomfortable, but it also means growth and change.

At one time, your partner seemed to fit your ideal or, more accurately, the current mutation in a lifelong emotional process. Our image of a suitable mate is a combination of childhood impressions, experiences, fictional models, and present needs. When we meet someone new, we compare him or her to the mental image we've created. He or she becomes associated with positive memories, values, experiences built up over time. Part of the process of leaving is to sever, or desensitize, the emotional bonds that have become identified with this person.

Being alone again—and it doesn't matter if you left or were left—means facing up to the fears that kept you cowering in a destructive relationship. You may be afraid of being independent, of loneliness, of alienation, or of isolation. You may fear rejection by family and friends, financial insecurity, or failure. You are stepping into the unknown, a place full of guilt, shame, and anxiety. You worry about the effects your decision will have on your children and the effects that the stress of acting unstressed will have on your health.

There are other terrors ahead. You know what breakups do to you, even when you instigate them. In the past you got depressed for months and cried yourself to sleep. Ending a relationship takes over your life for a while, and you just don't want to face that.

The future with a partner is risky enough. The thought of being alone brings on a rapid heartbeat and dizziness. But you've already learned that fears avoided are intensified. Not thinking about them preserves them, which suggests that they are unsurmountable. Confronting an anxiety reduces its hold, provides you with strategies for dealing with it, and desensitizes you to its emotional arousal.

There are any number of emotions and responses you can expect to experience as you consider leaving and then act to end a bad relationship. There will be a strong sense of pride, confidence, independence, competence, strength, growth, and freedom. You will feel lighter, freer, happier, and more optimistic than you can remember. These are the good feelings.

Depending on your history, circumstance, and situation, you will also probably have some bad feelings like anxiety, grief, guilt, anger, and loneliness to greater or lesser degrees. These are all natural feelings, too, the expected result of the dilemma you face and the uncertain outcome. Feeling bad, acknowledging a loss, and being anxious about the future are realistic, but temporary, responses to a transitional period. Understanding them and knowing what to expect reduces the intensity and frequency of these negative feelings. It also provides reassurance that they are passing clouds in an otherwise sunny and clear outlook.

ANXIETY

Now is the time to put the techniques of the past few chapters to work for you.

Find a quiet, peaceful place where you will be undisturbed

for a while. Visualize leaving your partner. Imagine telling him or her that you're leaving, then informing family and friends of your decision. Visualize yourself living alone. Pretend you are telling your children. Stay with each image, feeling whatever fear or anxiety that develops for a minute or so.

Keep track of your emotional reaction: heartbeat, breathing, forehead and neck muscles, dry throat, nausea. Are you light-headed? Dizzy? Do you have to go to the bathroom? Are your arms and legs rubbery and uncoordinated? Do you feel vulnerable? Powerless? Do you need to move, pace, rub your hands? By monitoring these signs of the arousal response, you can judge the intensity of your fear or anxiety.

If your responses become too strong, use deep breathing, exercise, and other methods for reducing stress described in Chapter Six. Remind yourself that you are just exploring your options, not committing to a plan of action. You are in a safe, secure place and you do not have to go any farther or feel uncomfortable any longer. Slow down, even stop, until you are again relaxed and comfortable.

Imagery works because the brain follows specific pathways in response to stress, regardless of the origin of the fear. The main distinguishing feature between sources of anxiety or fear is the intensity of the reaction. Big fears trigger strong reactions; little fears trigger weaker ones. Responding to threats is a key to survival, but you can learn to monitor the emotion-based reactions and use them for your advantage instead of fighting or ignoring them.

People show differing sensitivity to the physical symptoms of the arousal response. Some are upset by a thumping heart while others are more disturbed by the nausea. Often the sensitivities mirror family history: Early heart attacks, colon cancer, or asthma may lead to susceptibility to accelerated heartbeat, nausea, or rapid breathing. Recognizing that these symptoms are evoked by emotional upset may prevent a snowball effect. It can help to remember that horror films, competitive sports, and moments of great happiness bring on similar, and equally intense, physical reactions without signaling illness.

Explore the fears you associate with leaving your partner. Allow yourself to examine each issue carefully, and if it becomes too disturbing, stop and relax. It may help to repeat safety chants: I'll think about . . . , Now I'm going to consider . . . , I'll look at what it would mean if. . . . Use the phrases as reminders that you are just thinking about the future. None of this *has* to happen. You can control the direction and speed of the images and your thoughts.

GRIEF AND GUILT

Loss, even one you intentionally cause, triggers a grief reaction. Stress and chemical imbalances, as well as loss, can induce the same series of responses. Some people are predisposed to such reactions, possibly inherited to varying degrees.

Grief usually refers to the loss of a person, and it is essentially the same whether you leave or are left. Often the main difference is timing. People who are suddenly faced with a departing partner still have grief to experience. Those who leave mourned the loss of a relationship earlier and most recently have been feeling angry and victimized. After they depart, guilt takes over.

Following a universal human instinct for justice, someone who has decided to end a relationship looks for support from friends and family. Although some sense of guilt is unavoidable, an overwhelming feeling of fault suggests an imbalance. Use your outside sources to reinforce your decision. If your friends throw a party to celebrate your freedom, forget the guilt and get on with your life.

It can also help reduce guilt if you give your partner every opportunity to make changes. Be very clear and specific about what you want. Discuss your needs and be willing to listen to your partner's point of view. Get counseling. Follow up on suggestions. Do what you can to save the relationship—but remember that you're not obligated to wait forever. Don't let guilt manipulate you into an uncertain future.

You may be experiencing guilt because you always take the blame for anything that happens around you. Examine your feelings. Do you tend to be a martyr? Do you assume you were at fault in sidewalk mishaps, traffic accidents, or bank overdrafts? Clinicians call this internalizing, and it is the opposite of externalizing, which is blaming others for your mistakes. To avoid the guilt trip, seek out support from relatives, friends, or therapists and listen to them.

Some people try to avoid feeling guilty by provoking their partner into leaving. That tactic can create extra bitterness. Often, dealing with guilt is a matter of coming to terms with yourself and accepting your feelings. Did you delay making your decision because you didn't want to hurt your partner or because you didn't want to take the blame for the breakup? Are you acting to protect yourself or to hurt him or her?

Guilt is composed of three parts to varying degrees: fear—of being discovered, of having to face the person you hurt, or of offending your own moral standards; depression—sadness about the consequences of your actions as well as any losses that are involved; and anger—often at yourself for having violated your own code of behavior. Honestly evaluate your guilt. Although internalizers get along well with other people and have high standards for themselves, they are often too harsh about their failures and become discouraged at their inability to control mistakes.

Learn from past errors, but don't take on responsibility for the world. Not everything is your fault or due to your lapse, particularly in a relationship. You may be partly responsible for a bad relationship, but if you didn't have the intent to undermine it, then you shouldn't feel guilty. No amount of love, trust, loyalty, or stubbornness will change a sociopath, reduce the torments of the jealous, give a loner a yearning for people, or bring an abuser under control. Keep your sense of guilt in perspective and practice to reduce its unexpected appearances.

A woman may be responsible for an alcoholic husband's grief when she leaves, but she is trying to make the marriage work. It is his drinking and his attitude toward it that created conditions that forced her out. She needn't feel guilty about the decision to leave a hopeless situation.

Using imagery and friends, role-play your discussions with your partner. Begin with a clear description of your unhappiness. Listen to your explanations: "I'm not good enough for you." "You can get someone who is better for you." "I need more space." "I don't know how I feel. I just have to be on my own." "I need to get away." "It's not you. I just don't know what's wrong." These are expressions of guilt.

Try to think of the response and your reply. Confront your partner with your feelings. Give him or her every chance to change and consider your expectations. If the situation remains impossible, be clear and direct when you announce your feelings: "I have tried everything possible, but I am not happy in this relationship. It is best for me to leave. I care for you, but I am no longer in love with you."

This decision can be very difficult, but it is the best tactic. Holding out false hope for reconciliation is more destructive. Be prepared to pack and leave immediately. If possible, be packed before you announce your departure. It is okay to discuss your relationship and your feelings in a few days or weeks. Give your partner time to catch up to your perspective. Agree to counseling, consult family members, or follow any other suggestion, but don't stay if you've decided to go.

Guilt may be appropriate if you leave without warning, if you run off with someone else, or if you provoke your partner into leaving. Guilt becomes inappropriate when it overwhelms your life. If you become self-destructive or are unable to soothe your feelings, or if the guilt is long-standing, overwhelming, and immobilizing, then you may have a problem with self-worth. This often indicates undue responsibility for others' feelings, lack of awareness of your own emotions, and a poor understanding of the appropriate expectations in your relationship.

Don't let an inappropriate sense of guilt send you back to your partner when you don't want to go. If you're being pressured, ask what you can do short of resuming the relationship. Usually, our guilty feelings are a response to someone else's needs. Any decision to return has to be based on your best interests, not your partner's proclaimed need. He or she may have been just as unhappy as you were in the relationship but is feeling anxious about an uncertain future. Resuming a relationship that no longer interests you is a waste of time, energy, and emotion. It only makes matters worse and postpones the inevitable.

If there are children involved, be honest with them. Children often blame themselves for divorce and usually keep those feelings a secret. Kids believe in magic wishes, and making a cranky parent disappear surely meets some deeply felt anger. A small child may be sure his or her angry thoughts about a parent are the real reason for your separation. Discuss feelings with children and try to maintain a good relationship with them. Don't use them for revenge. Allow them the freedom to make their own decisions about each parent.

ANGER

Rage is a part of every dead relationship but rarely stays at a constant level. Usually, it comes in waves. A person who has decided to end a marriage typically experiences anger long before the decision is announced. Many people work through their anger over a period of months and even years before they decide to leave.

If you're angry with your partner, you have hope of change and improvement. You still have emotions vested in your partner's response, and that suggests the relationship is still alive. When that anger dissipates and you give up any hope of rectifying the arrangement, you will no longer have an emotional investment and you will feel justified in leaving. It is a cliché based on truth: Indifference, not hate, is the opposite of love. The partner being left knows rage after the move is made.

Anger is typically driven by a need to regain equality. If you feel that someone has harmed you, your anger is propelled by a need for revenge and a sense of balance. If you feel angry at your partner, ask yourself what is unbalanced, what you want from him or her. It can be anything from an admission of guilt to a change in behavior to material compensation.

One way to approach this is to ask yourself what it would take to eliminate your anger. If you can identify what you want, you may be able to negotiate with your partner. Articulating your needs can direct your anger more constructively. It transforms your anger into a goal, one that you can measure and know if you can attain.

A sense of unfairness often provokes anger. If you are angry at your partner, it is important to try to redress the problem, even as you are working to fall out of love. First, ask your partner for cooperation. If that's not forthcoming, ask yourself what will compensate you for the hardship you've endured. Look for ways that you can compensate yourself, since many partners will refuse to accept blame for your hardships.

For example, if your self-esteem is low and your job and social skills are weak as a result of the isolation imposed by the relationship, consider what is reasonable compensation. Perhaps a membership in a health spa, or tuition for career training, or financial security. Once you figure out what will compensate you for your anguish, you can begin working toward each goal. As you attain each one, your anger will diminish and your self-esteem and confidence will grow.

Just venting anger usually doesn't reduce it. It may, in fact, make it worse by drawing a target for your wrath. Since unfairness is usually the cause, reversing the situation and righting the balance is more effective.

Bill

Bill felt betrayed and humiliated when he learned that his wife, Denise, was having an affair with a coworker. She denied it at first, so he accused her of lying, infidelity, and broken vows. Bill was enraged, and the more he talked about it, the angrier he got. He became aware of more details, realizing that she had used his money, given to her as a gift, to buy her lover a present. He was obsessed with retaliating against the lover, and against Denise.

His anger and the thoughts of revenge took over his life. He was depressed and couldn't sleep. When he came in for therapy, I asked what Denise could do to reduce his anger. After a brief hesitation, Bill produced a list of demands: She must apologize; say she loved him; confirm it wasn't his fault; agree to try therapy to work on improving their marriage; and never speak to her lover again. Denise also agreed to support him to their friends. He agreed to do the same for her. She kept her promises, which resolved his anger, and they both worked at the marriage.

Acknowledging and analyzing anger can prevent the self-destructive behavior that only complicates an already stressful situation. Some people use their children to vent anger at a misbehaving spouse. That harms the children and increases the general bitterness. Others self-destruct from unexpressed anger—losing jobs, going into debt, becoming unreliable, and so on. In many states, counseling is required to prevent vindictive reactions if the parties to a divorce seem unduly angry.

Lawyers often become the targets of the rage generated when a marriage ends. Typically, one or both partners take out their anger at the opposing attorney, using their own lawyer as a surrogate.

Anger is an arousal-based response. Factors that enhance arousal will intensify anger. For example, if you're jealous, subject to peer pressure, or fearful, your anger will be more intense. Things that reduce self-control—such as fatigue, depression, alcohol, or drugs—facilitate anger.

Although both anger and anxiety are based on arousal, they act in different ways. Anxiety motivates you to back off, while anger encourages you to confront the situation. Some people use anger to overcome anxiety. Someone afraid to confront a partner may instead provoke him or her to anger. In the heat of the argument, the fears of confrontation are reduced.

When a relationship ends, one person is rejected and usually feels intense anger. The feeling of betrayal adds to the need for revenge and the sense of injustice. Anger occurs primarily when you feel victimized and there is someone to blame, even if it's yourself.

Feelings of anger tend to propel people into confrontations. Some therapists encourage people to express their anger as a way of coping with the problems and obstacles they are facing. It can be useful in helping people overcome fears and guilt to face the troubling issues in a marriage. Many people deny anger to avoid confronting a partner, but this usually builds resentment and adds more tension in the long run.

An excuse or limitation may reduce your anger. You may be willing to forgive someone who was drunk or sick, who apologized, who tried to make amends, or who truly tries to change. But the angry feelings intensify if you get no apology, if you are influenced by alcohol or drugs, or if someone is trying to take advantage of you. Other factors that heighten anger are support from a peer group, a lack of respect toward you, and your own history of getting angry.

Contrary to popular belief, expressing or venting anger does not necessarily reduce it. Venting is a firefighter's strategy in some situations: breaking open a window to vent, or let out, built-up heat. But it sometimes backfires by adding oxygen to an already raging inferno.

Venting anger can exacerbate things by enraging or hurting the target of your wrath without eliminating the injustice that is upsetting you. Some people are not comfortable expressing anger. If it's more important for you to be liked and to get along with others, venting rage may not be helpful.

Stating your feelings may make clearer what and whom you are angry at, but this can also intensify your anger by bringing it into better focus. Instead of a vague rage at a distant "they," you have a specific target for your unhappiness. If you can't get a response, your fury may grow. Anger is best subdued by corrective action, not ventilation.

Many men have difficulty expressing anger toward women because of the social taboos against attacking females. They may suppress their anger and try to ignore it. When an angry man leaves a woman, he is often reluctant to say how really furious he is, unwilling to violate the cultural barriers. He may never confront the real issues, which only makes the woman involved more confused and enraged herself.

Some women, in turn, are reluctant to confront men because it is not considered feminine to show anger. These women lack experience with intense feelings and are so imbued with an impossible ideal of comportment that any strong emotion terrifies them. A person who has avoided her feelings may begin to think her anger is unmanageable. She fears that any slip in her control will unleash emotions she will never again restrain. Other women fear violent retaliation if they force an angry confrontation with their partner.

Self-help or other supportive groups may not help with anger. Typically, the group's acceptance of your feelings redefines the target of your rage—it's not his drinking, it's him.

They also encourage you to express your anger. This could lead to your becoming more angry without doing anything to change the root cause.

Let's look at anger more carefully. If you are angry at your partner because he refused to stop drinking or lying, your feeling reveals several aspects about your perspective:

- You recognize that you're not in control. If you could control his behavior, you would do so and not be angry.

- You want something from your partner and assume he won't do it voluntarily.

- You have asked him to stop in the past and he has refused to.

- You are indirectly informing him that he has control, something he may need or want to hear from you.

- You have run out of options for dealing with the problem.

- You are making a negotiated offer: You stop drinking or lying; I'll stop bitching.

Ranting and raving can have unexpected results. They can intensify the feeling of injustice by spotlighting the issue. They also communicate that you are out of control. Some people are threatened by anger and do what is demanded to avoid facing someone else's wrath. Others become more resistant, sensing that the angry person is bluffing.

Some people use their anger to control others. If you are reluctant to leave because your spouse uses anger to manipulate you, there are some methods to help you handle it. To begin with, he would not resort to anger if he were not out of control and dependent on you for what he wants. He may have developed his rage to a high art for manipulating people and negotiating position. In essence, he is saying, Do what I want and I'll stop being angry. If that sounds like a bad deal, negotiate a better one for yourself.

Betsy

Betsy described her life as hell. She had three young children, a house in the suburbs, a good teaching job, and a husband who owned a small dental laboratory. But Tony had a nasty temper that he lost regularly. When Betsy tried to talk about his long hours at work or his lack of interest in the children, he got angry and walked away. If she raised questions about his friends or her lack of spending money, he went into a tantrum. To avoid his rage, Betsy stopped confronting him about anything.

That was just what Tony wanted. Knowing that Betsy would not ask any questions, he began staying away from home regularly, reappearing without warning. He denied gambling, until Betsy learned he had lost a lot of money at the racetrack. He was deeply in debt but refused to discuss it with her. She finally realized that he had used his anger to manipulate her. When she filed for divorce, she said felt as if she had been released from prison.

If you recognize that you are in control—he is out of control, remember?—you should also realize that if you accept his offer, you will almost always lose. People who use their anger to get what they want usually resent those who give in to their demands. Manipulators lose respect for enablers, believing they gave in out of fear and weakness.

Show some flexibility, but don't cave in to get peace. Parents quickly learn that appeasing whiny children only means more high-pitched, nasally demands later. Your impossible partner is still a whiny child in most ways.

After months of vacillating and ambivalence, you realize that your situation is hopeless and you are ready to leave. You have role-played the scene and are prepared for his reactions. You understand his anger and you expect to feel some guilt. Because you know what to anticipate, you are fortified. You can control the situation and restrain your emotions. You can leave knowing you tried to salvage the marriage but could not sacrifice your own mental and physical well-being for someone who was not offering something in return.

LONELINESS

The greatest thing in the world is to know how to belong to oneself.

—MONTAIGNE

Just as arousal reactions go back to primitive times, so does the fear of being alone. Humans are pack animals. For early humankind, cooperation and imagination were their main advantages over predators. Solitary humans were prey to any stronger animal that came along. Our fear of solitude remains, even though we've developed a culture and an economic structure that provide for singles.

Loneliness is often confused with depression. They both involve sadness, boredom, and lethargy. Following a loss, loneliness associated with the absence of gratification can lead to depression. But many people who are alone are not lonely; they have adapted to being alone and may prefer it. Separating loneliness from depression can simplify the solution. Depressed people tend to withdraw socially, while the lonely are eager to meet others and develop social contacts.

When loneliness turns to depression, the resulting tendency toward skepticism, cynicism, inertia, sadness, irritability, negativity, powerlessness, and futility may interfere with any efforts to reduce the loneliness. Typically, the depressive symptoms that accompany loneliness are the main obstacles to resolving the problem. Lonely people often spend their leisure time at the movies, gardening, reading, playing with pets, doing research or craftwork, or involved in other activities that don't encourage company.

Each person is responsible for his or her own loneliness. Why do you think you are lonely? If your answers are, "I'm not good enough"; "I'm not worthy"; "No one will like me," you need to be more considerate of yourself. Your lack of self-esteem and self-worth are undermining your own efforts.

Typically, people-pleasers are so concerned with the needs of others that they ignore themselves. They treat themselves as inferior and unworthy and eventually see themselves that way, too. To break the pattern, try treating yourself better. Consider your feelings. Focus on your needs. Notice when you are putting someone else's desires ahead of your own interests.

Long training and the habits of a lifetime are difficult to reverse. If you're having trouble, use some of the techniques discussed earlier to help. Reduce your fear of disappointing others by role-playing with yourself. Imagine a scene—perhaps telling your niece you can't baby-sit—making the arguments for everyone involved, including yourself. While watching TV, visiting with friends, or sitting at the movies, notice how others assert their needs. Use those scenes to embellish your role-playing. Try visualization and imagery to desensitize your fears, especially of rejection and loneliness.

You may be lonely because you are afraid of becoming attached too easily. People who have high separation anxiety, who have a strong need to be liked, or who find rejection or rejecting unbearable often show this. They feel they will be trapped without hope of escape if they commit to someone, so they avoid relationships. They don't have to face painful scenes, or happy ones either. If that's the case, you need to become more assertive, to give your own needs priority, and to deal with your fears of separation.

Someone with a fear of commitment or intimacy also may be lonely. These people are reluctant to make any long-range decisions. They often break off relationships when they become too serious. Fear of commitment and fear of intimacy often stem from low self-worth and low self-esteem. These people have to learn to like themselves enough to believe that someone else will like them.

The anxieties and fears that cause loneliness can be treated with the same techniques discussed earlier. They can intensify if they are ignored, but when they are confronted, they can be reduced and even extinguished. With imagery, slow breathing, and movement, you can face your fears gradually and at a pace you control. Eventually, you can work your way into actual situations and realize how unfounded your anxieties and fears are.

Visualization is often effective against fear of intimacy. In a comfortable, quiet place, imagine progressively more intense scenes of intimacy. Take your time and stop if you get uncomfortable. Visualize scenes revealing private aspects of your life, discussing your fantasies and dreams, involving sexual intimacy.

Many of the newly single are more anxious about intimacy than about loneliness. They can't imagine sexual relations with someone other than their former partner. In this case, it is best to use visualization in small, gradual steps. For example, focus on a pleasant, entertaining conversation with a date. Once you can picture that situation without anxiety, move on to inviting the date back to your home for coffee— from the front door, to talking on the couch, to a good-night kiss or more.

Take each step at the speed that makes you comfortable. If you get anxious visualizing undressing, for example, go back and imagine making more coffee. Gradually work yourself to the point where you can visualize foreplay and even intercourse. This technique takes time and patience but is remarkably effective for the newly single.

SELF-WORTH

A low sense of self-worth is at the root of many kinds of anxiety and loneliness. Most people base their self-worth on what they think are others' opinions of them. But those judgments are based on someone else's needs and issues. Someone who values intelligence, athletic ability, appearance, or success will judge you accordingly. Many of those attributes are gifts and don't reflect intentions or effort. They can change with time, experience, circumstances, and opportunity.

Psychologists typically use character as an indicator of someone's suitability in a relationship. Someone of good character is loyal, trustworthy, fair, reasonable, cooperative, and helpful—all qualities that are attractive in a partner. Relying on someone else's opinion means accepting his or her standards, which may not be yours. People value someone else's assets if that person has qualities that are needed. If you want security, you will value people who have achieved material success. If you want real friendship, you will value someone who is loyal and honest.

Unlike gifts, character can always be improved. If you lack self-esteem, examine your character. If it needs work, you can feel better about yourself by making changes. If it is already good, learn to appreciate your special qualities. Give yourself some room for mistakes—you wouldn't be human without them—and set your own standard of behavior for yourself, not some impossible ideal culled from romance and gossip.

Some people are lonely because they take on too much and set themselves up for disappointment or even failure. They blame themselves for anything and everything that happens. Although taking responsibility for errors can lead to constructive changes, overdoing it can be destructive. You get angry at yourself and the irritability makes you unkind, even punitive, further lowering your self-image.

The tendency automatically to blame yourself may make it difficult to show anger to others even when it is warranted. It may also make it impossible to accurately analyze what happened and prevent a similar mishap. Those around you assign unrealistic goals—they don't have to worry about not meeting them; you'll take responsibility—setting up more failure and blame.

Other lonely people never blame themselves; someone else

is always responsible for their misfortunes. People around these externalizers eventually become fed up with the lack of responsibility and denial of any fault. Someone who refuses to find a job but talks endlessly about low support payments and someone who complains about restricted visitation but won't pay child support are examples of externalizers who drive away potential friends.

It is important to consider your fear of loneliness carefully. Most likely, you are picturing yourself uncomfortably and conspicuously alone in a room full of strangers. The mind anticipates the worst and conjures up the most terrifying scenario as a survival tactic. But that nightmare of loneliness is a rare occurrence. Most often we are surrounded by acquaintances who can easily become friends if we make an effort.

Working through the emotional complications of ending a relationship bound by emotional ties takes effort and willpower. Moving on means leaving behind a history, years of commitment, and strong feelings about each other. For most people, the rewards of making the move more than outweigh the fleeting and flimsy negatives. Leaving a tension-filled, impossible situation is like starting life all over again.

Anticipating the uncomfortable moments ahead may make you nervous, but realizing you have the strength and technique to handle them should reduce your anxiety. It is worth doing, regardless of the obstacles, to save yourself, to regain your self-worth, to protect your self-interest, and to ensure your survival as a worthy, useful person. A life that restricts your growth is not living. It turns you into a victim, controlled by someone else's needs. Taking action, ending the relationship, leaving a marriage is an act of independence, growth, and survival.

♣ 10

Mad, Bad, and Dangerous
to Know

Unhealthy Relationships

𝔐AD, BAD, AND DANGEROUS TO KNOW" IS HOW LADY
Caroline Lamb described her lover, the Romantic poet Lord
Byron. Even Caroline Lamb, an eighteenth-century beauty
renowned for her wildness and stubbornness, eventually
conceded that Byron was untamable and hazardous to her
emotional health. The same can be said of the assortment of
rogues and futile attractions described earlier.

Adept at manipulating emotions and rationalizing behavior, these abusive types leave you bereft of self-esteem, self-
confidence, feelings, and freedom. Often, you were not aware
of how completely you were losing control, having been
focused instead on working out the problems in the relationship regardless of personal sacrifice. The priority is to appease
the demands of the abuser and not consider the long-range
effect of the abuse, whether physical, emotional, or psychological on you.

Abusers are controlling. That may include your movements, schedule, food, friends, and career. They are also
manipulative and self-absorbed. Whatever your involvement,
you don't really have a relationship with abusers. They use
you to meet their needs, not because they have any strong
emotional attachment. Abusers do whatever they can to make
you dependent and under their control, including lowering
your self-esteem, attacking your self-confidence, and demeaning your sense of self-worth.

In many cases, a series of small crises overshadow any larger apprehensions about an impossible partner. The doubts raised by one set of decisions get pushed aside while dealing with an immediate emergency caused by an even more questionable series of choices. With the information in this book, you may recognize patterns that reflect your own experiences. If you use the techniques described previously to reduce your anxiety, you may finally acknowledge to yourself that your partner is abusive and intractable. Knowing the source of the problem is the first step to severing psychological bonds with an abusive mate.

The key to breaking those bonds is to recognize:

❧ The past: Why did you get into the relationship?

❧ The present: What is it doing to you?

❧ The future: What will happen?

I discuss each of these issues as they pertain to the various types of rogues and futile attractions described earlier.

VICTIMS

Past

The victim's partner usually believes the victim's chronic complaints and does what is possible to help. You don't realize that the care and devotion are counterproductive and allow the victim to deteriorate rather than improve.

Further, you may have a strong need to help others and may suffer from low self-esteem. People who end up with victims try to build a relationship on the victim's appreciation of their devotion and self-sacrifice. Instead, the victim's feelings of indebtedness lead to resentment, aggravating the problems. By focusing on the victim's problems, you avoid facing your own.

Present

To break free of this bond, it is necessary to look carefully at the relationship in its present state. Despite long nursing and devotion, the victim is not improving. His or her demands continue to be selfish and manipulative. Indebtedness and guilt are not a basis for a healthy relationship. In fact, catering to the victim's perceptions of weakness is destroying both your lives. To break the cycle, you must respond differently to your partner's helplessness and chronic complaints.

Anyone who projects blame onto others to avoid responsibility is being manipulative and abusive. Once you recognize that your offerings are being taken with no expectation of giving back, the psychological bond can be broken. It is based on commitment, loyalty, and devotion, qualities that have been lost in the manipulations, selfishness, and abuse that characterize these relationships. Victims show little interest in or respect for your needs. You can help break the cycle by recognizing that permitting a victim to maintain that role and avoid responsibilities only perpetuates the problem.

Future

Good at suffering and usually depressed, victims respond with warmth and love when nursed and supported in their troubles. Most partners eventually find such a relationship static, starved of growth as it becomes fixated on the victim's needs. Usually the caretaker ends up frustrated by the lack of effect, bored by the lack of growth and variety, and depressed by the lack of change. If you are an enabler and remain in a relationship with a victim, you will probably become more and more restricted because your life will be limited to your partner's boundaries. You will become more dependent on the abusive victim as the rest of your world dwindles.

MR. EXCITEMENT

Past

Often the woman who chooses Mr. Excitement also is addicted to a hint of risk. If she were more cautious, she wouldn't continue to seek men who are always in trouble of one kind or another. Like him, you may have believed there's clear sailing ahead if you can just weather one more storm.

An eternal optimist, Mr. Excitement always assures you of his ability to overcome the current obstacles and have a normal life. If only you will wait just a little longer, he says, it will all come together. Surely you're not going to desert him now. The expectation plays on your guilt and loyalty.

Many women feel more secure when a partner is dependent on them to support him in trouble, even if it is to pay his bail. He may acknowledge other women but describe you as "the special woman" in his life, his only close relationship. Professing loyalty, he relies on you to pay bills, keep track of legal matters, provide him with food and shelter. His admission that no one else would put up with him gives you a false sense of security.

Manipulative, he will make you feel disloyal if you talk about leaving. You may even share some of his illusions about risk and responsibility. Or you may be living vicariously through his antics. None of those reasons needs trap you in an abusive relationship with Mr. Excitement.

Present

It didn't take you long to discover that your life is a series of thrills with no substance in between. The relationship depends on his quest for excitement, not your life together. Whenever you fix one mess, he gets into another. This is addictive behavior with no development or future and with constant pressure.

You probably also recognize that Mr. Excitement is abusive, manipulative, and deceptive. He shows none of the commitment or loyalty that you show him. The constant stress is debilitating, weakening your health from cigarettes, alcohol, drugs, coffee, sleepless nights, anxiety over legal and medical problems, isolation from family and friends. In short, he has a life—and you don't.

Future

Do you have children? Do you have time for them? What about your career? Do you still see family and friends as often? Is your health good? Does he ever ask about your problems? Do you lend him money?

Typically, this relationship ends one of three ways: a major crisis or accident; you get dumped for someone more exciting and less complaining; you finally wise up and decide to leave.

You can bring spark to your life without him. A strong career or a healthier relationship with someone else will provide plenty of excitement, chaos, surprise, and confusion. Life doesn't have to be on the brink to be exciting, interesting, and joyful.

CONTROLLERS

Past

All controllers—perfectionists, bullies, and brutes—need to dominate because they really feel inadequate, insecure, and inferior. They are vulnerable and are terrified of being found out. People who are comfortable with themselves and feel secure don't need to dominate.

Controllers try to shift focus onto you, blaming you for all of the weaknesses they feel. By making someone else feel inferior, inadequate, and insecure, controllers' fears are alleviated. For example, perfectionists will accuse you of being disorganized and incompetent rather than admit their own fanaticism and self-doubts. Felix and Oscar in *The Odd*

Couple are a perfect example of the competing sides when a perfectionist is half of the pair.

If you live with a controller, ask yourself why. Are you happy? Are you staying for the children? Are you living on hope? Have you lost your self-respect while you were accommodating him or her? Are you isolated and lonely? Have you been able to think for yourself?

People who live with controllers prefer having decisions made for them. They often confide that they fear being alone or getting a divorce. The controller plays on your feelings of loneliness, guilt, and loyalty.

Present

Staying with a controller doesn't help either partner. Controllers are caught up in a delusion: If only you would do what they want, everything would be okay. But even if you were perfect, they would find a cause for complaint to keep the spotlight off themselves.

If your partner is violent, you and your children could be hurt or even killed. Controllers have limited capacity for caring; otherwise they wouldn't be abusive. They are not committed to anyone else and don't deserve loyalty. They use people with little thought or concern.

Future

Life with a controller is a never-ending slide into desperation and despair. For a while, you may believe that if you can only meet your partner's demands—be more organized, more accountable, more careful, more thoughtful, more helpful—life will improve. But perfection buys only a brief respite.

Controllers continually make escalating demands, isolating you from family and friends. They hope to cut off all of your ties and support and make it more difficult for you to break free. Restore your lost contacts slowly, making each one another step in your recovery.

Breaking free is an ongoing process of small steps, each

relatively easy to take, not one huge leap for freedom. It is easier for most people to think of such life-changing actions incrementally. The mind tends to catastrophize, focusing on the worst possible outcome. As a result, many people resist change because thinking about it is too frightening. Considering each step individually reduces that anxiety.

Once you clearly understand that your partner is a controller and a healthy relationship is impossible, then the psychological bond will be broken irreparably. Over time, the drinking, temper flare-ups, violence, health problems, and so on will get worse. If you stay, you will lose even more of your self-esteem. As you deteriorate, your partner will lose respect for you and see you as weak and inferior, justifying more control over you.

JEALOUS PARTNERS

Past

Jealous partners accuse you of infidelity at inappropriate times and get you caught up in proving yourself. By constantly attacking you, they deflect attention from their behavior. They isolate you from family and friends and are preoccupied with their accusations and need for reassurance. The one-note conversations prevent the relationship from developing.

Present

Jealous partners are abusers. They devastate your self-esteem and self-confidence. Being in a relationship where you are constantly on the defensive and blamed for everything around you is very destructive to you and to your children.

Future

Nothing satisfies jealous partners. Often they become dependent on your attempts to quell their suspicions. You may even become dependent on their unceasing demands. Jealous partners won't change unless faced with an ultimatum, and often they need therapy to deal with underlying anxieties. It is difficult to break old habits and establish a new relationship based on shared interests and trust. Most people in this relationship eventually lose hope of damming the unending stream of anxieties and leave.

MOOD SWINGERS

Past

Mood swingers' bad moods usually don't last long enough for them to acknowledge. Instead, they see themselves as good-spirited and energetic in their up periods. Often, they blame any bad moods on you. You spend your life trying to accommodate their demands, but the more you do so, the more they find something else to complain about. So you just go through the motions and try to keep your mind on hold.

Present

As with other impossible partners, living with mood swingers leads to low self-esteem; feelings of inferiority, insecurity, and inadequacy; lack of personal development; and isolation from family and friends. But there are even more low points.

They make you question yourself, wonder if you're sane. They insist that they are generally in a good mood; it is only your carelessness that makes them angry. It usually takes time to recognize a true mood swinger, so many people question their own sanity before doubting their partner's overactive response.

You get depressed because nothing ever works out. First there's a burst of energy, but complications and lack of planning usually slow it down until the mood swinger gets frustrated and angry. In time, you grow to hate the euphoric stage because of the inevitable disappointments.

You feel frustrated, tied up inside. Any attempt at talking

to mood swingers is rapidly upended, with you getting the blame. Because outsiders usually see mood swingers when they are up, family and friends find your mate charming and take his or her side. That leaves you feeling isolated and even more vulnerable to attempts to blame you for problems.

You may develop health problems such as stress reactions or gastrointestinal disturbances, or begin smoking or drinking.

Future

Mood swingers don't expect things to last, but they hold on for as long as they can. If you stay, you make accommodations out of fear of the bad moods and your partner enjoys the power and control. If you sabotage the relationship, your partner may leave first, claiming to have lost all respect for you or that your arguments drove him or her away.

Often, mood swingers' partners feel sorry for their mates; they always seem to have bad luck. Your departure will make things worse. True, life has been a series of disappointments, but that's not your fault. They refuse to change and reject any compromise, preferring instead to feed off your guilt. Mood swingers need professional help, and even medication.

LONERS

Past

Loners are very attractive. They don't cheat or stray; they don't even socialize. They are so grateful to have a relationship that they don't jeopardize it. Partners of loners are either like them or trying to rescue them. This is usually not possible, because the presence of another person reduces the loner's need to make changes. Often both people have similar fears of abandonment and develop a symbiotic relationship.

Present

You may be tired of the self-imposed isolation from friends and family. Loners discourage your growth and development, afraid you will outgrow them. Their detachment can impair the development of children, as well as the growth of your relationship.

Future

The longer you stay with a loner, the more dependent you become on him or her. Because your own skills deteriorate, you may feel that your options are limited and you are trapped. Eventually you may become so bored and tired by the lack of growth that you are ready to leave.

DEPENDENT PERSONALITIES: MOLES

Past

Partners of moles seek security. Moles accommodate every need, and this is irresistible at first. The selfless generosity seems to be out of love, but it really masks strong insecurity and a deep need to be wanted. You may enjoy the adulation. It is unlikely that you also are a mole, since similar types tend to avoid each other. Ambitious men, for example, often choose dependent women to handle hearth and home while they are building a career. When success is achieved, the dependent, and now older, woman may be replaced with someone more independent, resourceful, and youthful.

Present

Moles bore most partners with their dependency and lack of variety. You get tired of making all of the executive decisions. Meanwhile, you lose the respect of family and friends who think you take advantage of your dependent spouse, who looks like a saint to everyone else.

You find your worst qualities exaggerated and hardening. You become more self-absorbed with the encouragement at home. You rely on your partner's dependence, making all the plans, keeping track of appointments, taking responsibility. You also assume that your needs and wishes always come first and must be accommodated. Regressing, you may lose your ability to control impulses, venting anger whenever something vexes you. As a result, healthy relationships with friends and family become difficult if not impossible.

You may also feel lonely because dependent spouses never seem to offer an opinion or response. Even when they do say something, it is always the same, so it amounts to nothing. Your complaints often get little support from others, and you come off looking selfish. After all, nobody looks good with a mate on a leash.

Future

Eventually, the need for feedback and response tends to drive a mole's partner to infidelity, especially since you have become alienated from family and friends.

A mole rarely ends a relationship and tolerates enormous amounts of emotional abuse to keep one going. The longer you stay with a dependent personality the harder it becomes to leave. The habits of control, selfishness, and egotism are hard to break.

PASSIVE-AGGRESSIVES: SABOTEURS

Past

Saboteurs seem accommodating and pleasing at first. You don't realize that they stockpile resentments, expressing the resulting anger through subtle actions and attitudes—always being late, never offering a straight compliment. You may not recognize the pattern immediately and blame your own actions instead of the passive-aggressive personality.

Saboteurs are very insecure and refuse to acknowledge anger or discuss their own needs. With no idea of how to express anger and terrified you will leave if they try, they deny their emotions. They try to be cooperative but can't break the pattern.

Present

Disappointment and frustration are daily experiences. You try to second-guess potential problems. Inevitably, you become resentful, and your partner is baffled by your attitude—he or she didn't purposely forget to set the alarm, didn't mean to put the red socks in the laundry with all your white shirts. It must be your problem.

Eventually, you may feel as if the relationship is driving you crazy. You question friends, but they are unsure who is at fault; your partner seems so nice. You feel trapped and may even get physically ill—headaches, tension, stomach problems, and the like. Family and friends may avoid you, tired of your complaints, sympathetic to your partner, annoyed by the bickering. The absence of growth depresses you, and everyone feels your irritability.

Future

You find yourself confused, hating your partner one minute, feeling sympathetic the next. You question your own actions and feelings. You can't decide whether to divorce, enter therapy, or stay put.

Ultimately, you will probably leave. The relationship lacks a core of love and caring and fails to grow. The resentment of both partners consumes all other emotions. Arguments are useless and eventually stop. You recognize that you remain only from habit; all emotional ties broke long ago. Even when you are ready to leave, the saboteur's resistance will make it difficult.

PERPETUAL ADOLESCENTS

Past

Many women are attracted to the youthful, carefree nature that this type projects. Seemingly unaffected by the normal problems and concerns, he makes you feel young again. You are happy living in the present and ignoring past problems and future obstacles.

Adolescents' partners are often like themselves, rebelling against authority and responsibility. You don't want to act mature or postpone gratification. You are proud of your spontaneity and impulsiveness. You may love living vicariously through his adventures and secretly enjoy his refusal to conform to social standards. You look forward to his acts of defiance. They are distracting and an interesting diversion from other problems.

If you live with a perpetual adolescent, the chances are you don't handle stress well and avoid it at all costs. Like him, you try not to overdo the demands on your time. When stressed you become moody and frustrated, so you act irresponsibly, if necessary, so that others won't expect too much from you. You may skip a meeting without calling, or fail to return a phone call.

Your partner lifts your depression and eases your anxieties. Unlike other impossible types, he isn't controlling or critical. You both laugh a lot and spend time together. The relationship is intense, if shallow, but you try to forget that and concentrate on now.

Present

Over time, you will grow up and yearn for more substance. The relationship lacks growth potential, relying on endless parties, hangouts, and pranks for excitement. You end up cleaning up the messes, resolving unpaid bills, and taking care of whatever practical problems develop.

You feel cheated and abused. He refuses to commit to anything and you realize you're not important to him except as an escape from responsibility. He refuses to grow up and you come to feel depressed and lonely when you're with him. His friends come first in his life and you resent their constant presence.

His lack of interest in your world can alienate your family and friends. He ultimately makes you doubt yourself and reduces your self-esteem. If you yearn for him sexually and emotionally but are repulsed by his selfish, immature behavior, you begin to distrust your own judgment. You can't help feeling good around him, even though you know you shouldn't. It's like an addiction, and your internal arguments don't seem to help.

More questions about your behavior arise. Why don't you ask more from him? Why are you so desperate? Why are you so fearful of rejection? Why do you tolerate his abuse?

If you become angry at his indifference, you may want to hurt him to get even. When you do, his lack of understanding reduces your satisfaction. You try to control him, expending time and effort. Over time, you realize life is passing you by. You long for something better and feel even more depressed because you habitually neglect yourself to take care of him.

Future

Without growth and change, the relationship dies. It may be killed when he is arrested for driving while drunk or if he runs out of money. He may find a better playmate or just decide to move on anyway.

Or you may make the first move, tired of his childish games and loser friends. His pranks suddenly will seem pathetic and you will realize that nothing ever changes with him. He will resist if you try therapy.

Because he doesn't antagonize, you may find it difficult to leave him. If you try to provoke him, he'll just avoid you. He insists he loves you and promises to mend his ways. He makes it difficult to sustain anger and you may leave several times before the final break. When you do leave, you will feel depressed and angry at yourself for taking so long to get out. After all that time with a child, your self-esteem will be low.

SEXUALLY INCOMPATIBLES

Past

Unlike the other futile attractions and rogues, gay men aren't intrinsically unsuited for a long-term relationship—just not for a relationship with a woman. But some women find homosexuals very appealing, perhaps because they are more likely to share some female interests and passions, anything from cooking to art to fashion. They also understand the importance of relationships. Studies show that women and gay men put a higher priority on relationships than straight men.

In most cases, the relationship is established without either of you acknowledging his preference. Gays still face legal sanctions, cultural stigmas, and other disadvantages, and some prefer to experiment with alternatives. He may want children or a high-profile career. Some straight women knowingly marry gay men hoping to change them or thinking they won't mind the sexual limitations.

Present

The problem with this relationship is the deception involved. The man is living a lie that eventually spreads to other parts of the relationship. If you didn't know when you started, when you discover the lie, it destroys any hope for trust, fidelity, or loyalty.

Even if you did know of his preference from the beginning, the stress of limited sexual satisfaction and the inevitable infidelity dooms the relationship. You are in constant doubt, wondering at every absence or delay. The free-floating anxiety may bring about headaches and insomnia and almost always causes depression and an enormous drop in your self-esteem. The limited physical intimacy causes you to doubt your adequacy. You feel rejected, but he denies any coolness so you blame yourself.

Future

Over time, the uncertainty, distrust, and lack of a sexual bond alienates you. Although life together started out safe and secure, the absence of sexual tension eliminates an important catalyst for creativity and change. With no growth or development in the relationship, you feel dissatisfied. Your partner is more like a roommate, and your self-esteem plunges.

A survey of therapists showed that the couple with the least chance of survival was that in which one partner is straight and one is gay. It is rare that either changes orientation, and problems abound. Friends and family are often disapproving. If you try therapy, most counselors advise against a reconciliation.

HABITUAL LIARS

Past

Impulsive and charming, habitual liars are not easily discovered. Many people find themselves hopelessly in love and thoroughly entangled before realizing that the new partner cannot be believed. Liars have learned that the truth may mean a long wait or hard work, while telling lies often brings quick results and an easy solution. Because honesty plays such a limited role in their thinking, they resolve problems and overcome delays only temporarily. Until they are discovered, habitual liars are well liked, expansive, and carefree.

Actually, these people feel too inadequate and uncertain to be truthful. They don't know how to face life without lying.

Habitual liars lack confidence but maintain a superficial optimism. They deny problems, avoid stress, and look for surface solutions. Uncomfortable with in-depth analysis, the habitual liar circumvents the truth to evade trouble whenever possible.

Present

Anyone involved with a habitual liar catches on to the deceit sooner or later. Then you feel abused and betrayed. The realization that the entire relationship may be built on half-truths and outright lies destroys trust, confidence, and loyalty. Some people become overly sensitive to all untruths, even socially condoned lies.

Usually, once one story unravels, the whole fabric shreds. You are numb at first, then furiously angry. You probably want to get back at the liar. It takes months to recover, and the experience can color all future relationships. Lies have a long half-life, undermining trust and confidence for years.

Once found out, habitual liars still look for a quick and easy fix to their problem—your forgiveness. This gives them what they want, an unobstructed path through trouble. Nothing has changed. They go on using lies to avoid responsibility.

Future

Before you decide that a liar can be saved, remember, your partner deliberately lied to you. His or her agenda was more important than your trust. This has happened countless times in countless ways. Typically, you discovered the lie; liars rarely confess.

To test a liar's avowed willingness to reform, suggest a long, complicated reconciliation, one that involves time and effort. For example, you could ask your partner to start therapy, to make a detailed review and accounting of all previous lies, to offer reparations to everyone involved, and for outside verification of all of future questionable claims. Chances are the liar in your life will decline to participate.

EGOTISTS

Past

People attracted to egotists never get much attention. If you are living with one, you may be trying to distract yourself, avoiding your own feelings of inadequacy, insecurity, and inferiority. Or you may be a rescuer who wants to help people with problems. The egotist is delighted to get the attention and has an unending supply of troubles that need help. Your mate provides you with something you want, and you give him or her every second of your attention.

Egotists are good at disguising their selfishness, so it can take a while to discover their weakness—for themselves. Their jokes about self-absorption may hide their seriousness, and their praise for your attention may mask their selfishness.

Present

Egotists are the center of attention. They demand your devotion and your constant involvement. Over time, your own interests wither away, your skills dwindle, and your development regresses. To check this, ask yourself: Have I recently made new friends? Have my old friendships expanded? Has my career changed or grown?

Your apparent lack of concern for yourself may be reflected in the reactions of family and friends. Many of them may feel that your mate is taking advantage of you while losing respect for your lack of self-esteem. That can alienate you from friends and isolate you from your family. Eventually, the closing off of your life will be an embarrassment even to the person who encouraged you to shut the doors.

Future

As with all things, egotists blame your decline on you. They also fault you for alienating friends and family, for adversely affecting their image, for lacking ambition, for being too dependent. The process snowballs with attacks on your insecurity and lack of confidence. With your self-esteem a casualty and your sense of self-worth long gone, you become more dependent and clingy.

You grow increasingly anxious and insecure as the years pass. Depressed by the stagnation and lack of gratification in your life, you become more dependent. If you try to overcome the depression by finding something who attracts your interest, your partner will feel threatened by the outside distraction. You will have to choose between your own development and focusing your attention back on your partner. Often, the long-established fears and anxieties, the habit of dependency, and the sense of inadequacy are difficult obstacles to overcome.

Eventually most egotists leave, having lost interest in their depressed and dependent partners. They may complain that you are no longer sexually attractive and an embarrassment in front of their friends. Or they may just seek alternative sources of gratification. You tend to chores and other daily needs while your partner spends more and more time away from home without excuse or explanation.

Some people find the chronic anxiety and depression unbearable. If that's your situation, your attempts to help yourself may antagonize your partner. You have to leave to help yourself to break the psychological bonds and get on with your life. But don't expect an egotist to change. From his or her point of view, why tamper with perfection?

You have learned enough to reach a decision about your partner. If your mate fits one or more of the personality types described, your relationship will probably follow the pattern outlined. Instead of waiting passively for the inevitable, you can act to save yourself and improve your life. Using the techniques of imagery to desensitize your anxieties and confront your fears, you can prepare yourself to escape from a dead-end relationship and move into a more exciting, productive, and self-confident period of your life.

☙ *11*

Having It Your Way

A Search for Greener Pastures

𝓛OVE. COMMITMENT. TRUST. LOYALTY. CONCERN. CAR-
ing. Devotion. Sharing. Sexual excitement. Intimacy. Passion. Support. Faith. Friendship. Understanding. Values.
Affiliation. Approval. These are the elements of a healthy,
mature, and lasting relationship between two adults. As in
the well-known fast-food jingle, you can have it your way—
with some, none, or all of them. If your current relationship
is missing some of these ingredients, it is your decision to do
without, try to add them, or move on to something new that
provides more choices.

Perhaps your partner is not as hopeless as the rogues and
futile attractions, but you may still feel that the relationship is
at a dead end. As explained in Chapter Eight, relationships
are held together by behavioral, psychological, and/or emotional ties. The previous few chapters focused on the emotional bonds, the most difficult to break. This one discusses
how to escape from a relationship based on behavioral and/or
psychological ties.

LEAVING

Even if you're not facing an imminent physical threat of violence, life with an abuser of any kind is deadly to your self-
esteem, your self-confidence, and your self-worth. Moving
on—and out—is the only sure way to save yourself and regain your sense of security and control.

It may help to remind yourself that falling out of love is a process you can control according to your needs. It has several steps, but they are all part of the system developed to help you confront survival threats.

When you first consider leaving a relationship, you will probably ruminate about the alternatives. Allowing yourself to do so, using imagery and the other techniques described in Chapters Six and Seven to reduce your anxieties, gradually eases your fears. You become desensitized to them and better able to handle real problems. By controlling the time and place of your exposure, you can speed up or slow down the process and your desensitization.

You may experience a sense of loss as you consider ending a relationship. Imagery and other visualization can help you with that, as well as with fears about independence, loneliness, responsibility, job hunting, or other problems. When you realize you are concerned about only your situation—finding an apartment or getting a job—the ambivalence process is completed. You have faced up to the anxieties and vague fears and are ready to strike out on your own.

If you still feel anxious and uncertain, you may have more work to do with imagery and desensitization. You probably need more exposure to and visualization of your fears in a safe, untroubled place. Some people rely on positive thinking, refusing even to think about anxiety or fear. But if you refuse to consider your nervousness about living alone, for example, you will never reduce it, only encourage it to grow unchallenged.

Some people say that the discussions on anxiety and visualization are unnecessary. For them, ending a relationship is just a matter of willpower. They'll move on, they believe, just as soon as they are ready. But willpower is a short-range motivator. It is not meant for falling out of love, a long, drawn-out process filled with negative feelings like fear, depression, shame, guilt, and rejection. That requires a more gradual, progressive approach that allows the time and effort necessary to recondition responses.

The vacillation of the ambivalence process can be uncomfortable. If it bothers you, slow it down and take it one piece at a time. Or ask friends for support. Keep in mind that this process works best if given time. If you need goals to keep going, encourage yourself by identifying your progress. Make a list and cross off items.

Magical insights don't work for the long haul. Most people have residual positive feelings for a partner and fears of going it alone when a relationship is ending. That's why it takes so long to make the final emotional break. There are lots of steps sideways, even backward, while making forward progress.

Think of the desensitization of your fears as a continuum. Whatever your current state of mind, you are somewhere in the middle. You can decide how fast to go. You control the process; it doesn't control you. As you learn to use it, your self-esteem will soar. If you let your fears take over, you will feel a loss in self-esteem. To improve your feelings about yourself, spend more time and effort using visualization to desensitize anxieties and face your fears.

If you choose a confidant to help you, be judicious. Confidants are often neglected after problems are solved. You may be uncomfortable continuing to see someone who knows so much about your emotions or who has heard many negative things about a partner with whom you reconcile.

BREAKING BEHAVIORAL BONDS

Some couples stay together out of habit or from social pressure, forgoing the intimate and pleasurable aspects of love for the behavioral bits and pieces of a long-standing, if no longer devoted, partnership.

Both partners in such a relationship really live separate lives. They may share household chores, even expenses, and appear as a couple to the outside world, but there is no depth. In many cases, they no longer feel any particular loyalty or commitment. Often, one or both are involved sexually with someone else. Frequently, they no longer share values or beliefs or interests beyond the immediate living situation.

One example of this is an older couple who have developed individual interests and friends. They do chores and share finances, but nothing more, not even arguments. Their lives are so disconnected that they have no emotional response to each other.

An abusive partner also can create this kind of situation. You may interact with the abuser, but out of dependency, not love. Often you have lost all emotional concern but face financial or physical problems that make leaving difficult, if not impossible.

Or there may be no abuse, just a need for the other person—for financial support, child care, housing, family problems, illness, or some other cause.

Other circumstances that can lead to a relationship held together only by behavioral bonds include falling in love at first sight before a friendship can develop. When the passion dies, there is nothing left. Or two people who are opposites may be attracted briefly. Sometimes, meeting someone during an emotional crisis leads to a relationship that can't last when the emergency ends. Examples of this are couples who meet when one or the other is rebounding from a previous relationship, or who come together during wartime.

In any of these situations, one or both partners come to feel that the relationship is unbearable. They are bored or no longer in need of whatever bond kept them together. The lack of a caring, concerned partner and a deep, fulfilling relationship may become more obvious after the children have grown. Or perhaps one person has found a new love, or finally recognized that the difficult partner will never change.

People stuck in relationships tied primarily by a behavioral bond often view them based on the costs versus the benefits. As the situation changes, so does the ratio, and they act accordingly.

If the above description sounds familiar, you may be

trapped in a relationship based only on behavioral bonds. To be sure, try to imagine leaving your partner and ask yourself the following questions:

- Would I feel threatened discussing leaving with my partner?
- Would I feel ashamed telling family or friends that I am breaking up?
- Am I afraid to live alone?
- Would I miss my partner?
- Am I angry at him or her?
- Do I have a strong need to be perceived as morally right or to get revenge or be vindicated?
- Do any of these images evoke an emotional reaction?
- Have I felt any guilt, anxiety, or anger while thinking about these things?
- Do I share any interests, values, beliefs, attitudes, or personality characteristics with my partner?
- Do we feel any loyalty to each other?
- Are we sexually exclusive with each other?
- Do we share similar attitudes toward each other's roles and responsibilities toward each other?
- Do we see each other as similar?

If you've answered no to most of the above questions, your relationship lacks both psychological and emotional ties. It is based mostly on habit, behavior, situation. You may be ready to move on but don't know how or what to do about it.

Because your relationship is probably based on a cost-benefit analysis, you may only have to find a better alternative to motivate you to leave. If that's your situation, it may help to make a list of what is good and bad in your relationship and think about the alternatives available to you. When a relationship is based on behavioral bonds, there are neither emotional—fear, anger, hope, guilt—nor psychological—commitment, loyalty, trust, friendship—factors to keep you involved.

Usually, people caught in this predicament are struggling with lack of motivation, lack of exposure to better alternatives, and/or lack of awareness of the risks of staying as they are.

Some people need motivation. The longer you wait to make a move, the more settled you become and the more difficult the changes are. If you don't get out, your dependence on your partner increases, creating psychological ties as well as behavioral ones. Staying in an empty relationship puts your self-esteem and potential at risk.

If your partner is physically or emotionally abusive, think about the effect on your children. If they are not victims, they are still being damaged by what is being done to you. They may turn into abusers themselves. In an abusive relationship, the risks of staying are always more dangerous than the consequences of leaving.

A bad relationship sours your expectations and creates a negative outlook on the future. Consider joining a support group to help you through the difficult emotions.

Breaking off a relationship based on behavioral bonds demands new alternatives. You may have to expand your circle, tell family and friends that you're available, look for new contacts, perhaps take courses in an adult education program. Some people pursue long-ignored interests like bird-watching, square dancing, cooking, or drawing.

The advantage of these options is that they engage your attention. It is always better to be truly interested in what you're doing, not just using it as a means of meeting people. That will come as you get out, but if you are enjoying yourself, you will be that much more attractive and interesting.

You will be at your best, and if you happen to meet someone, you can at least be sure you have something in common.

Another advantage of taking a course or enrolling in some program is the new skills you learn. They may be enough to allow you to be financially independent, further cutting your need for a dead-end relationship.

If you're not sure what you want to do or learn, contact a local college, university, or mental health center. They can provide vocational tests for determining aptitude, achievement, and interest. Self-help books may also offer ideas. For those with skills and background, just getting a job can widen their horizon and provide income.

For those with special problems, a vocational rehabilitation office can help determine if you qualify for funding. They also offer support to anyone who is disabled, handicapped, or in need of other special assistance. If you're concerned about your own or someone else's drinking, you might consider joining Alcoholics Anonymous, or Alanon for family members of alcoholics, or some other self-help group.

You might want to try taking out an ad in the personals section of a newspaper or magazine. This is often very effective. Because ads often generate a lot of answers, be prepared to screen people. Set up first meetings in a public place—a restaurant, museum, or park.

Be honest with the people you meet. Tell them whether you're looking for a commitment, a casual relationship, or a friendship. Ask lots of questions about them, where they work, what they do, families, friends, and interests. And expect them to question you as well. You both have to learn about each other before deciding if you want to go farther. Don't forget to be on the lookout for rogues and futile attractions so you don't get caught again.

In general, it's best to get out of an old relationship before beginning a new one. The above suggestions are just to remind you of the many alternatives available to you. If you get too involved before the old one ends, you may find yourself in a very complicated situation. Ask yourself if you're relying on a new friend only for support and encouragement during a difficult period. Do you have anything in common? You may find that the new relationship breaks up once the old one is resolved.

BREAKING PSYCHOLOGICAL BONDS

Relationships held together by psychological bonds fall between those based on behavioral factors and those dependent on emotional ties. These couples share trust, commitment, loyalty, sexual exclusivity, friendship, attitudes, values, and even personality traits. It is the difference between friendship and romantic love.

The psychological bond in a relationship includes many of the characteristics most of us associate with love, among them:

- Caring for the welfare of the partner
- Trust and commitment to each other
- Shared values, beliefs, interests, and attitudes
- Dependence
- Gratification
- Support
- Acceptance
- Appreciation
- Self-disclosure
- Shared goals

Missing are passion and shared activities. These partners have separate behavioral agendas and lack passion but are held together by a sense of commitment to each other or shared values and beliefs. They may be compatible, even dependent on each other for emotional support, but both may be lonely, even bored and yearning for more. Or one person in the relationship may recognize that despite emotional dependence on the partner, he or she is really better off, in terms of personal growth, without the other. Someone who is married to a father figure, for example, may realize a need to develop her own identity separate from a protective and even stifling spouse.

People in this kind of relationship often describe it as loving but not being in love. It can be very stable and long-lived, but it is susceptible to a breakdown if one of the psychological ties is severed. For example, if one partner discovers the other has had an affair, the loss of trust and dependence can destroy the commitment and support necessary to continue.

If you are in this type of arrangement, you may decide to get out when:

- Trust is broken after an affair.

- Something comes between you, for example, a professional move that benefits one but is disadvantageous for the other.

- Your perception of your partner changes—you discover a gambling habit, a significant or radical change in religious belief, or abuse of the children.

- You reinterpret behavior, seeing your partner as manipulative instead of caring.

- You realize the relationship is futile because your partner is a hustler, is unable to commit, or doesn't really love you.

- Your partner becomes abusive.

- Your partner becomes addictive, develops emotional problems, turns out to be a liar.

♦ You realize that your partner wants to control you.

♦ Your partner is exploiting you, preferring to live on your income instead of finding a job, for example.

♦ Your partner's need for excitement endangers you.

Because this relationship is not fully satisfying, you may want to leave it. Usually you are not doing much together and there is no passion left. Your partner may be more involved in control and covering up his or her own insecurities and inadequacies than in participating in a relationship that allows you both to grow and develop.

In some cases, the abusive partner may be subtle, making you increasingly dependent, undermining confidence and self-esteem, alienating family and friends, playing on fears of loneliness and abandonment. Often what seems to be love turns out to be, on closer examination, manipulation, control, and abuse. Recognizing this is often enough to break the psychological bond. Once you realize that your partner and your relationship are destructive and not in your best interests, it is usually easier to make the break.

Sometimes a relationship is based on needs that were once important but no longer are. This is true of people who meet during wartime, emergencies, or other emotionally charged circumstances. When the crisis is over, so is the relationship, which has no depth to sustain it. For example, someone you meet during an election campaign for a favorite candidate may lose magnetism once the votes are counted.

Or a rescuer, someone who looks for people in trouble, may find there is no basis to continue a relationship once the partner overcomes his or her problems. The rescued person may continue to be dependent and needy to sustain the relationship.

The courtship doesn't always explore the differences. You may marry a workaholic when you expected to come first. Or your partner may want you to work when you want a more traditional family. You may want a dynamic lifestyle, filled with parties and social events, while your spouse prefers to stay close to home and is satisfied with a limited social life.

Many people find a choice made on the rebound takes odd bounces. For example, Paula divorced her alcoholic husband and married a teetotaler. But she learned that they didn't have much in common and his avoidance of booze was not enough to sustain a marriage. Or someone escaping an abusive relationship may next choose someone who is gentle and indecisive, too indecisive.

Whatever the circumstances in your relationship, if it is bound by behavioral or psychological factors, you can make the choice to leave. If you find it unfulfilling, static, controlling, or manipulative, you can explore alternatives and make new choices. You don't have to settle for a marriage or relationship that doesn't provide you with joy, love, security, and growth. You can have it your way. You just have to broaden your outlook and make the decision.

☙ 12

Down but Not Out

Rejection, Depression, and Anger

𝒥T'S OVER. THE RELATIONSHIP YOU WERE TRYING SO hard to keep together is ended. The partner you loved has left and you're alone.

Most of us react to the departure of a lover the way we respond to death. Someone is gone from our lives, and we experience grief. Like many other emotions and responses, this is part of a process developed over thousands of years as part of the human condition.

Early humans took the death or disappearance of a companion seriously. This was not so much for the person missing as for those left behind. The group's response to any loss assured those remaining that each one was an important and necessary part of the whole. The time spent searching or grieving was proof that every individual was vital. It strengthened the social bond and boosted the morale of everyone, knowing that every absence would be noted and mourned.

As a result, the grief reaction is a universal human response to loss. Other species—monkeys for example—grieve in obvious ways (they appear sad, mope around, and don't eat). But some animals, like zebras, quickly adjust to the death of a member (think of nature films where zebras return to grazing while lions devour one of the herd). Grieving is also one of the main social bonds among human groups. And although there are minor social variations depending on religious or cultural customs, some characteristics are universal.

I have found from my research and practice that the feelings triggered by any significant loss in one's life follow the same pattern each time. Knowing what they are and how they affect you can help you cope when you are going through the process.

ALARM

This is typically the first reaction to a loss. The mind tries to find ways of reversing or undoing it. In extreme cases, or if circumstances are unusual, mysterious, or doubtful, the mind may even deny the loss. For example, a wife confronted with only circumstantial evidence of a husband's infidelity may refuse to believe it. This can help reduce the shock at first, but if the denial continues, it interferes with her ability to cope with the reality, and that is detrimental.

This stage is more arousal than depression. The person who suffers the loss becomes mobilized and focused, directing enormous energy and concentration toward overcoming the loss. Often, he or she resists advice to give up these futile efforts. The arousal response insulates us from becoming depressed and allows work on resolving the loss.

Sometimes it goes too far, as when someone refuses to believe a love affair is over. I treated one man who refused to believe that his fiancée really wanted to break up. One day, he forced her into his car, threatening to drive out of the state with her. She finally convinced him to pull over so they could talk. Taking advantage of the opportunity, she escaped from the car and went to the police. He was arrested for kidnapping, but the charges were dropped when he agreed to therapy.

PERCEPTUAL ADJUSTMENTS

When the desperate efforts triggered by the alarm stage prove unsuccessful in reversing the loss, people typically make perceptual adjustments to try to reduce the importance of the loss. If your partner has left, you may try to ease your pain by insisting you will find someone better or by recalling your ex's flaws. You may convince yourself you were never really in love or that you were ready to leave anyway. If those feelings are true, they can help lessen the sense of loss. But if they are not real, those attitudes can raise obstacles on your road to adjustment and recovery.

One woman refused to allow herself to feel any grief when her boyfriend never called after an argument. She just insisted he was a jerk and not worth caring about. By avoiding the grief process, she delayed her own recovery. A year later, she admitted that she was still angry with herself for starting the final argument and she still longed to be with him.

Denial

Denial is a relatively unsophisticated defense. Often it causes frustration for family and friends who are angry when you apparently refuse to accept the obvious. That can cause resentment, especially if they attack you. Under those circumstances, no one is helped.

Compensation

Some people try to offset the loss by neutralizing it. This is what happens when you jump into a new relationship immediately, and why those rebound romances so often fail. Or you may take up a new activity or treat yourself to something you've always wanted. This can help, as long as you understand what you're doing and why. But relationships or interests based on a need to compensate for a loss can't be judged on their own merits and often fade over time.

Positive Thinking

This adjustment can be helpful if done with understanding and perspective. When faced with a dead relationship, it can be useful to find a silver lining—new freedom, new possibilities, less stress and tension. It encourages you to keep hoping, motivates you to find new sources of gratification, and generates a good attitude that appeals to those around you. Obviously friends and family would prefer you to be upbeat and hopeful instead of depressed and morose.

But if your positive attitude and belief that you will easily find a new partner keep you from examining the old relationship, it can be detrimental. The philosopher George Santayana said that those who forget the past are condemned to repeat it, and that holds true of your personal past as well as the record of world wars and civil revolutions. If instead of trying to understand what went wrong and making changes, you just keep going in your old fashion, that sets up a repeat situation that could leave you very lonely.

A second problem with positive thinking is the mental energy it requires. It takes a lot of reinforcement from friends and from yourself. That energy could be better expended looking at your problems and trying to resolve them, not on an unrealistic optimism about happy endings down the line.

Finally, positive thinking can make you rigid and closed to alternatives. People who insist that everyone adopt their perspective can become self-righteous and narrow-minded. For example, a woman who insists that if she takes a positive attitude, her husband will give up his girlfriend, refuses to consider that this may not be the first or last time the husband is unfaithful. This kind of blindly positive thinking can close you off to other alternatives.

Repetitious Thinking

As explained earlier, the mind tends to place the highest priority on the most important problems. If your lover has left, you will find yourself dwelling on your loss. This kind of thinking serves a number of purposes. First, this may aid you in trying to reverse it. One woman was stunned when her husband of fifteen years asked for a divorce. He said she was so preoccupied with the children that she had no time or interest for him. She denied his accusations at first, but when faced with the end of her marriage she started thinking about it day in and day out and began to see his point. She agreed to work on correcting those problems, and he agreed to give the marriage another try.

A second purpose is that dwelling on the loss can also be a valuable tool in helping you learn from your mistakes. Often, the lessons learned from the process are profound. They can be among the most important discoveries in your life. People rarely analyze things when they are happy and enjoying life. It is only when you are unhappy that you look around for ways to make things better. As a result, most of us learn and grow as a result of the losses we experience and the lessons that come from them.

By repeatedly examining and replaying the circumstances of a loss, you gradually become desensitized to the pain and anguish it brings. This process—repeated exposure—is very similar to the imagery technique discussed earlier to desensitize fears. In each case, it is the exposure that helps. Avoidance or distraction only perpetuates the fear or the pain.

Lynn did everything in her power to prevent her lover from returning to his wife. Her preoccupation caused her to alienate her friends, who could no longer stomach "Dave this" and "Dave that." Yet, after a while, Lynn's images of Dave became less vivid, her emotions less intense. The recollections of weekends making love grew duller and tarnished by the reality that Dave had chosen his wife over her.

Repetitious thinking, by itself, could easily take many months to desensitize a major loss. Further, it can be very disturbing and disruptive. Over time, the need to focus on the loss and the pain it brings can lead to depression. As explained previously, although you can distract yourself from unhappy and unpleasant thoughts for short periods, the need to resolve a problem means that your mind returns to the loss until you find a resolution. This also brings anguish, reminding you constantly of what you no longer have. To protect itself from the emotional pain, the mind slows down, and that is the basis for a depressive reaction.

Recent studies have shown that the mind regulates the speed and energy available for thinking by adjusting fluids, called neurotransmitters, that lie between nerve cells in the brain. During the alarm stage, there is an increase in the neurotransmitters that facilitate or speed up thinking, thus enabling you to deal with the crisis—either to undo the loss or encourage conflict resolution. If no solution is found, and you are caught between the opposing needs of repetitiously thinking about the loss and finding a distraction to reduce its anguish, then a reduction in the neurotransmitters acts to ease the pain. This drop in energy level leads to a depressive reaction. The loss continues to receive high priority, but to minimize the anguish, less energy is available and the speed of thought is reduced.

Depressive Reactions

This is the slowdown of psychological and motor activity, allowing you to handle the process of thinking about the situation, the past, and the future. The sluggish thinking and acting means you are limited to basic activity, reducing interest in new things. It is as if your mind has decided that things aren't working right, so the best choice is to slow down and make the necessary corrections before resuming your normal level of activity.

Someone having an extramarital affair may face the same situation. After the first rush of passion and intensity, the frustrations and problems mount and reduce the initial gratification. This loss of satisfaction and pleasure can trigger a depressive reaction. The resulting slowdown will force a decision since the person will no longer have the energy to maintain both relationships.

Or the depressive reaction may bring a person into therapy, realizing that he or she has to deal with the problems. Depression itself can be therapeutic, and ignoring it, forcing yourself to look on the bright side, is inconsistent with what your mind is trying to accomplish.

For some people, the misery of a depressive reaction is the goad they need to take action. Their fears of loneliness, financial insecurity, or whatever have locked them into a destructive relationship, and it is only when they become depressed and go for help that they find the strength to break free. Often, the feelings of helplessness and hopelessness that accompany depression free them to say and do things they would not otherwise do.

Helen hated her marriage but felt overwhelmed with guilt. She could not imagine causing her husband pain by leaving him. Over time, she became so depressed and apathetic that she lost her previous interest and concern about his needs. She began to see his requirements as self-indulgent and was able to overcome her guilt about causing him pain.

Although depression can be productive if it encourages you to seek help, it can be counterproductive if you allow it to deepen and take over your life. If the depression interferes with sleeping and eating, it can affect your work. It is best to see a medical doctor or therapist if you are experiencing a severe depressive reaction. That way you can learn to deal with your problems and find solutions to your situation instead of suffering.

It can also help to be aware of outside influences that can worsen your depression. For example, being surrounded by reminders of your ex can drain you of the energy you need to get your life together. Old friends, too, can be helpful or hurtful. If they keep you stuck in your old patterns, they may hamper your recovery. If they are willing to encourage you to try new interests and outlets, they can be a positive force.

One very effective recovery tactic I have developed is to put aside a few minutes a day to concentrate on your depressive thoughts. After a couple of weeks, you will notice that allowing your mind the freedom of those few minutes lets you concentrate on other things for the rest of the day. Try to restrain the depressive thoughts to that period and focus on moving forward the rest of the time.

Desensitization techniques discussed earlier are effective on depressive reaction as well as anxiety. For example, if you think about the good things in the lost relationship, you will desensitize yourself to them, just as listening repetitiously to a piece of music eventually dulls your enjoyment of it.

Normally, people spend much less time focusing on a loss than they suspect. One woman told me she thought about her ex continually throughout the day. Yet, when she actually observed the pattern of her thinking what she reported was that the upsetting memories lasted no more than a few seconds at a time, totally only a few minutes a day. She found that even brief exposure to the loss triggered distractions and avoidance responses. You can easily set aside that amount of time in one or two compartmentalized periods each day, or you could devote more time to hasten your recovery. Allowing sadness to wash over you like a wave, knowing the tide will turn, can also give you a sense of control over your grief.

Try to spend time with each issue that raises a response. Take them slowly, trying to imagine all possible reactions. If your lover walked out, for example, you might imagine asking why he left. Go through every possible answer and your response to it. Be aware of what upsets you, what rouses an emotional reaction. Gradually, even those issues that were most upsetting when first considered will lose their thorniness.

One point to note: It is important to use imagery to desensitize positive as well as negative memories. After being rejected, some people focus only on the anger and frustration they feel toward the ex. When those extremely negative feelings are eventually desensitized, the person is left with only positive memories.

At this point you are tempted to get back in touch with an ex. You are receptive to apologies and advances and may even agree to resume a relationship with an abusive partner.

To break the cycle, Pauline tried to remember those romantic evenings with her lover as well as the anger she felt at his infidelity, self-absorption, and lack of any real interest or care for her. She imagined the best and worst of times with him and felt less inclined to invite him back.

As you confront the issues that bother you—whether fears of living alone or just loneliness—the techniques of repetitious reliving and exploration imagery will gradually desensitize your emotional response. Then you can deal with your circumstances in a logical, practical, and unemotional manner.

Movement and activities can also bring relief. Exercise, even just walking, can help. So can a support group. Remember, if you don't face your fears and anxieties, they will never go away.

SOME BASIC DOS AND DON'TS

Some images may be too painful at first, like your ex with his new wife. If you think about it too soon, the anguish may be discouraging. But the technique can be effective when used gradually.

Don't masturbate to fantasies of your ex. That just intensifies your feelings—reinforcing positive emotions around him or her—when you want the opposite effect. Even friendly conversations can be counterproductive when you're trying to fall out of love.

You're sure it's over. You've been desensitized and no longer like him nor fear being alone. So why not see him again? A phone chat seems encouraging and you make plans to meet. You've both cooled down, the memories are sweeter, and a rendezvous for coffee makes sense. While you're remembering the good times, don't forget the reasons why you left.

Emotions feel like forever. That's why being happy feels so great—and why everything looks so hopeless when you're depressed. But don't despair. Life only looks hopeless. Emotions do change and you will feel better. To get a sense of progress, don't consider your overall emotional state. Think instead about how you've reacted to the same issue over time. That's where you'll see changes.

FORGIVENESS

One of the most difficult aspects of getting on with your life after a relationship has ended badly is letting go of your negative feelings. For example, if you were living with an abusive partner, it is important for your self-esteem that you get an apology. That will also bring you new respect. If the apology is sincere and your ex is willing to admit a problem and the abuse, then it is to your advantage to forgive him and move on with your life.

Your ex may agree to the apology and admit the problem but also want to continue your relationship. If so, be prepared to make demands that go beyond a glib mouthing of "I'm sorry." As explained in previous chapters, that takes a real commitment and effort on his or her part.

If your partner is sincere, suggest compensation for yourself that would make you feel things are even. You might, for example, insist on a change of attitude, an end to drinking or drugs, openness and honesty, and definitely treating you with respect and affection. That means an end to all abuse, verbal as well as physical, and no more efforts to isolate you and alienate friends and family. It also means being supportive of your efforts to get training, find work, or whatever else you desire.

It is quite possible—often necessary—to forgive exes without any help from them. You may also have to forgive yourself, too, for staying with your ex for so long. Remember, what you are looking for from your ex you can give yourself: renewed respect, a commitment to change, and recognition of your own needs.

At first, you will have to watch closely, monitoring everything he or she does. If your partner keeps the promises and follows the suggestions you make, you will want to reconsider your position after a while. If not, be prepared to end the relationship and move on immediately.

This course of action will be difficult for both of you, but it is necessary to establish respect. An abuser may believe he or she loves you, but he or she doesn't respect you. Love without respect is worthless. Demand and secure respect and real love, based on trust, equality, partnership, and commitment.

If your ex is sincere about wanting to continue the relationship, he or she will be willing to compensate you and admit mistakes and problems. Those who want a quick, effortless return to the relationship haven't changed and aren't worth the time and energy. It is also helpful to remember that abusers are typically manipulative and many are incapable of change. Some will try to talk you into resuming the status quo.

TO SEE OR NOT TO SEE

After a breakup, many people have a very strong urge to see the former partner again. If you were the one who moved on, you may be feeling guilty and want to be sure he or she is okay. Calling or meeting briefly may alleviate your guilt, but it can backfire. If your ex was unhappy about the breakup, your call can raise false hopes that all is not lost.

You could find yourself back where you started, in a relationship that took years to escape, because your guilt and loneliness make you vulnerable to facile promises. That, in turn, can make you disappointed, even angry, at yourself. You have again placed his or her needs before you own.

To avoid the trap, give yourself time before making that call. Develop a new life, new friends, and new interests. Once you have established your life and independence, not bounded by loneliness and guilt, then you can check in and see how he or she is doing without you.

If you are the person who was left, you may be very dependent and hopeful of getting back together. Seeing your ex again may help to convince you that the relationship is really over. Some people, using fantasy and denial, convince themselves that things can work out after all. Sitting home alone, depressed and lonely, they talk themselves into believing everything will be all right if they can resume contact.

Meeting with a former partner can quickly dispel those delusions. Or it can turn into an addiction. Even if every meeting brings another rejection, you manage to get gratification from the contact with your ex. You may, for example, convince yourself that he or she still cares about you since he or she spends time talking to you or agrees to meet with you. If the two of you just talk long enough or meet often enough, the relationship can resume.

When the urge to call becomes overwhelming, it is important to ask yourself three questions.

Do you need your delusions broken or confirmed? Calling or making arrangements to meet should resolve things quickly and decisively. Usually after a separation of four weeks or so, it is difficult to reestablish the relationship. The person who left has become adjusted to living independently and is less inclined to return. There are always exceptions, of course, and meeting your ex again can indicate if there is any hope.

Are you acting like an addict? Are you obsessed with your ex, even though you know the relationship is over? Calling him or her hurts you, subjecting you to more rejection and even humiliation. It is self-defeating and against your best interests, and your healthy side knows this, but you can't stop the addicted side from picking up the phone. The good side is humiliated more and more, damaging your self-respect. Eventually, you welcome the rejection as punishment for your transgressions.

Do you accept the pain and anguish of continued rejection

just for the quick thrill of talking to him or her again? These are signs that you are growing dependent on the contact. Each time you call, the addicted side gets stronger and the healthy side gets weaker. You are reinforcing the addicted side of yourself, becoming insensitive and indifferent to the warnings from your healthy side. You are also becoming enured to the rejections. The urge to connect is gratified by the indulgence, regardless of the outcome.

If your addiction is based on emotional drives, you have to work at overcoming the emotional bonds that developed in the relationship. To do this, it will help if you recognize that you are displaying four negative characteristics: stubbornness; the need for instant gratification; the need for control; and self-absorption.

You are stubbornly refusing to develop alternative sources of gratification. Perhaps you think your ex is unique and irreplaceable. Perhaps you are unwilling to settle for less. In truth, a decent relationship, or even a mediocre one, is better than continual rejection. Or you may think you were the cause of the soured relationship and are punishing yourself. Or you are trying to prove your love with your addictive behavior. Another possibility is your uncertainty and doubt about your ability to meet someone new. You need to work on your feelings of self-worth with friends, a support group, or therapy. Or you may just want what you want. Is that a pattern in your life? Have you been equally persistent in the face of other rejections? Are you used to getting your own way all the time?

If your ex left you, your insistence on seeing him or her reflects your hope of starting up again. You have received unmistakable signs that it's over, but you'd rather have the instant high of seeing him or her, even with the pain and rejection, than the longer effort of starting a new relationship. That is one of the main lures of this kind of addiction, the instant and sure satisfaction from seeing the former partner.

Finding a new partner involves a long-term commitment of energy and time with no assurance of a reward anytime soon or anytime at all. Seeing your ex provides a quick gratification. But quick gratification carries a huge price. Just as drugs and alcohol offer a fast release from problems, they eventually create larger troubles. If you could get instant gratification from something—anything—there would be no incentive to pursue long-term goals. In time, your life is impoverished and narrowed, dependent on your source of instant satisfaction. That's one of the main components of addiction.

We rarely have total control over the things that bring us gratification. Whether at work, at home, or even in the gym, we cannot completely control the results of what we do. This can be very frustrating. But you seem to have control over your contacts with an ex-lover. You decide when to call, send a letter, set up a meeting. This stands in stark contrast to other areas of life.

This is very appealing. But the illusion of control is one of the main characteristics of an addiction. If you are frustrated and disappointed in other areas of your life, the sense of control you feel from maintaining the illusion of a relationship with your ex can be irresistible. But something that is irresistible is not subject to control.

The more you entertain the delusion that your ex will take you back, the more the other areas of your life wither. You could lose friends. Your work will certainly suffer. Your relationship with yourself will deteriorate as you lose self-respect. In time, you will be alone with your delusion. Rather than expanding and enhancing your life, your fantasy has constricted and impoverished it. This, too, is an important characteristic of addictive behavior.

If the above descriptions typify your relationship with your ex, there are several steps you can take to overcome your dependence on a dead relationship:

❥ Review the previous sections on breaking physiological bonds. As you become desensitized to your ex, the urge to make contact will abate.

❥ Recognize that the addictive components—stubbornness, instant gratification, need to control, self-absorption and isolation—are very destructive. Learn to distinguish between illusion and reality.

❥ Try to develop new sources of gratification. Make new friends. Test new interests. Join a support group. Go out with family, friends, or coworkers. Expand your horizons and your contacts.

❥ Work on developing a better relationship with yourself. Enhance your self-esteem with the techniques discussed earlier. Recognize that you are the most important person in your life. Monitor and regulate your values and priorities, keeping up an inner dialogue. Remember that the rejection and failure you experience whenever you see your ex punish, and diminish, your healthy side.

❥ Start slowly and work gradually. You are making big changes, and that takes time, effort, and energy. Don't expect a straight line. It moves in fits and starts, often taking one step backward to every two steps forward. Change is difficult and takes commitment.

REJECTION AND GUILT

Being left is painful and difficult to get over. Rejection is made up of several emotional responses in varying degrees, including fear of abandonment, depression associated with the loss of a loved person, anger at being hurt and perhaps even deceived and betrayed, and guilt related to feeling partly responsible. To overcome rejection, you have to deal with each component. You can use the techniques described previously to overcome fears, depression and anger.

Guilt is usually based on a sense that you violated a standard of conduct or did something wrong. If it's your own ideal, you may want to examine your motives and behavior. If you really feel strongly about it, you could consider some means of atoning. Whom did you hurt? How much? Why?

As you identify the specific causes of your guilt—perhaps you provoked your partner or had an affair—ask yourself what you can do to make up for it. An apology? An admission of your responsibility?

People often confuse guilt with responsibility. If you didn't assume your responsibilities in the relationship, for example, recognizing and acknowledging this can be beneficial. It is best overcome now through a commitment to change.

Visualization techniques can help with guilt. Imagine admitting your mistake to your ex and the response. Go through all possible reactions and your answers to each. Imagine expanding the discussion, asking your ex what it would take for forgiveness. As with other anxieties, imagery can desensitize your reactions to guilt and help you work on overcoming the feeling altogether.

SEXUAL PROBLEMS

It is common to experience sexual problems when a relationship ends. This is due, in part, to your familiarity with your former partner and the threat associated with any new relationship. The anxiety you feel may cause your body to turn off the sexual response just as it reduces your appetite. This is part of the fight-or-flight response discussed earlier.

When you find a new sexual partner, you may experience even more anxiety. To overcome this, practice the imagery and techniques discussed earlier. As with other fears, your sexual anxiety will grow if you don't confront and desensitize it.

The best approach, as I explained, is based on gradual, progressive visualizations. Follow this with a similar slow approach in reality. If a sexual problem persists, you should check with a physician to be sure there are no medical reasons for your problem.

Anger can cause sexual difficulties, especially if you are getting over a bitter, unhappy breakup. Unresolved anger can inhibit the expression of more positive emotions, including sexual arousal.

Depression—notorious for its negative effect on arousal—may also be a factor. The depressive response results in lowered energy, reduced drive, and ambivalent motivation, all of which lower sexual interest. Further, the irritability, negativity, skepticism, cynicism, and argumentativeness associated with depression can have a repressive effect on your partner. Who wants to go to bed with a grouch?

Another possible cause is guilt. If you have a need to punish yourself, it will restrict your willingness and ability to experience pleasure or even allow yourself to indulge in pleasurable activities. You may feel you're not worthy of the joy and excitement sex can provide.

Rejection makes people feel unloved, unlovable, and unworthy as well. These, too, can impair your sexual interest. You may be angry at yourself for being rejected. Refusing or denying sex may be a way of punishing yourself or restricting your indulgence.

Shame also brings a fear of intimacy. If you were humiliated in your previous relationship, you may not be able to experience pleasure. Or the sense of shame you feel may cause strong anxieties that inhibit your sexual interest.

As with other anxieties, imagery can help you overcome these feelings. To help yourself, follow these steps:

1. Imagine something nonthreatening involving a date with someone new, such as dinner in a restaurant.
2. Intensify the scene, perhaps dinner in your home with a date.
3. Role-play these images until your anxiety disappears.

4. Intensify the image with physical contact.
5. Each time, role-play the steps until you no longer feel anxiety.
6. Repeat the process imagining a real partner, going slowly and gradually until you feel comfortable with each step.

As you use the imagery, role-playing, and the other techniques described in this book, you reduce and eliminate the anxieties you feel, whether about sex, loneliness, or finances. These techniques can also help you overcome the loneliness, depression, anger, and rejection you may feel if you've been left after a long relationship. As I explained, they will take time, effort, commitment, and energy, but they can help you overcome these negative emotions and put your life back on a path to happiness, satisfaction, and pleasure.

In the course of this book, you've learned to identify the problems you are having with a partner, to foresee the future difficulties, and to master your anxieties about the end of that relationship. It is possible to fall out of love and to land on your feet, ready to take the next step to find happiness, commitment, and a satisfying, fulfilling relationship.

Putting It All Together

Case Histories of Treatment

𝒯HE EXAMPLES IN THIS CHAPTER ARE A GENERAL guide for using imagery and the other techniques detailed in this book. Every situation is different and dependent on the experiences, emotions, and expectations of the individuals involved. On the other hand, because so many failed relationships are caused by impossible personality types with predictable characteristics, the aftermaths also follow patterns. In many instances, a person anguishes endlessly over whether to leave an impossible partner. The rumination is a way of avoiding action. For most people, the how-to of leaving is more difficult than the why. The four case histories offered here illustrate alternatives and solutions discussed earlier, showing how real people put theory to practical use.

Ann and the Egotist

At forty-two, Bill, a successful lawyer, found himself increasingly depressed. He considered his marriage to Joan, an elementary school teacher, happy, but he also felt trapped. His work was no longer rewarding or challenging and had no hopes of getting better. Changing jobs would mean a pay cut, not something a man with two teenage children could afford. As it was, he could barely manage any savings.

Personally, things weren't much better. Bill thought the kids took too much of Joan's attention, and her job took the rest. His life was in a rut, dragging on from week to week in a monotonous blur. He was struck by his inability to differentiate the previous ten years, which were marked in his mind only by the children's development.

Along came Ann. Bill was attracted immediately, probably by her beauty, but originally she wasn't interested at all. She worked at the law firm, and they spent a year together on a major case. It had been tied up in the courts for five years already, and they used to joke about its futility and endless fees. Just staying up with the daily developments was a full-time occupation.

Somehow, they managed to find time for leisure. Bill was rejuvenated by their affair. They would schedule breakfast meetings and spend the rest of the day together. Occasionally, there were business trips or even weekday trysts.

For six months, the affair was dynamite, then Ann got serious. She wanted Bill to leave his wife. Bill, uncomfortable with her demands, refused. He felt betrayed by her change of attitude and intensity. He would make promises to her but never followed through on them.

The end came when they took a vacation together at a Caribbean resort. Ann wanted to explore and shop; Bill wanted to sit by the pool and drink. After nearly two and a half years, if they weren't in bed, they had nothing in common. Bill got irritable and Ann got cranky. When she went on a shopping spree at his expense, Bill blew his top. After a furious argument, they broke up.

Ann arrived in therapy determined to get over her love for Bill. She had had endless discussions with family and friends about their affair and how impossible he was. Ready to acknowledge that her apparent uncertainty was just a way of avoiding action, Ann moved quickly past why she should break up with Bill and considered how to do it.

The first step was to help her understand the bonds between two people and see how they matched her relationship with him. Ann realized that there were no psychological ties, and only a few behavioral and emotional ones, mostly related to sex and their work.

Next she acknowledged the pattern their affair had followed. Bill felt trapped by his marriage, his job, and his financial obligations. He felt unappreciated by family, friends, colleagues, and coworkers. He experienced the lack of change and growth in his life as loss. The sense of loss was as great as other losses that trigger a depressive reaction. Opportunity and convenience fed the affair. They worked together, had flexible schedules and free time, and he had a trusting wife.

But their goals and objectives differed. Bill wanted an indulgence, whereas Ann wanted a serious, committed relationship. Bill wanted an affair to supplement his life, whereas Ann wanted someone to share her life.

As a result, the affair had developed typical problems.

Bill set target dates for telling Joan about Ann—junior high school graduation, the end of a work project—but never kept his promises, insisting "he just needed time." He made token offerings to give the impression he meant to be with Ann: buying furniture she chose, getting a home equity loan to buy the vacation condo that was to be their home, giving her jewelry. He also blunted Ann's anger with flattery, insisting he was miserable without her and telling her she was prettier and more sophisticated than his wife. At the same time, Bill exaggerated his "good" relationship with his wife to assure Ann he was worth having. (Some men picture a wife as hopelessly ill or describe an abusive wife tolerated for the sake of the children to get the same results.)

The need for secrecy about the affair meant Ann could no longer seek advice from family and friends. She became isolated and more dependent on Bill. He denied being controlling, yet he got angry whenever she brought up the subject of his plans. He controlled the affair from the beginning.

Ann was fed up with all the unkept promises and was ready

to break the bonds. She saw how Bill's behavior followed the pattern of the classic egotist.

He was manipulative, deceiving Ann into thinking he wanted a serious, committed relationship when all he wanted was a fling. He manipulated his wife, through anger, to get the time and freedom to indulge himself. He also lied and intimidated to get what he wanted, even boasting to his friends about having the best of both worlds.

Over time, everything got worse: the lies, the procrastination, the manipulation and intimidation, the self-absorption, the irresponsibility.

Ann had tried to get Bill to change, to recognize her demands and respond to them. He refused to tell his wife and children about Ann and rejected any effort to change the relationship, to become more responsible or to share power with Ann. She recognized that the future with Bill was hopeless.

Therapy and a support group helped Ann. She learned how typical Bill was and how predictable his behavior was. Other people offered their own experiences with egotists, reinforcing the pattern and predictability of these relationships.

For Ann, the next step was acknowledging how destructive the affair had been to her. Her health had declined, probably because she wasn't eating or sleeping much. She was depressed, lonely, feeling out of control and isolated from family and friends. She suffered from low self-esteem, a sense of desperation, and a lack of growth in her life.

She began to take action, filling her life with new interests and activities. She reached out to her family and old friends again. Because they worked together, Ann couldn't avoid seeing Bill, but she was determined not to sleep with him again. She reminded herself how many times he'd lied and disappointed her. He wanted to start up again, but Ann wanted it over with.

Imagery techniques proved effective. Ann used them to

confront her anxieties about every aspect of her life and relationship with Bill. She began with the easiest and least intense scenes with him and gradually worked through everything that upset her.

To break the emotional bond, it was necessary for Ann to work on her fears, especially her fear of Bill's anger. She progressed through a series of scenes. When an image became too stressful, she switched to one that was less difficult. Gradually, she imagined scenes with Bill being apologetic, then annoyed, and finally antagonistic. Ann repeated scenes, frequently reversing roles in them, or facing other fears, such as living alone.

She began by imagining that she told him how upset she was with herself for having difficulty handling the delays in their relationship. She asked him if he was upset with her. He was kind and generous in his replies. She imagined him a little upset, then even more so. Then she reversed roles with him.

Ann imagined her friends confronting her for not facing up to Bill. So she imagined herself confronting him, and him confessing that he would never leave his wife, admitting he was selfish. Gradually Bill bared his soul, revealing his true intentions. Bill was with her, then with his wife. She was happy, then sad and alone. She was living with family, then with friends, then alone. Her life was good, then there were problems, then it was stressful.

Now Ann imagined that Bill reversed himself and left his wife to move in with her, then went back to his wife. She was depressed and heard him say he loved her, knowing he was lying. Then he said he cared about her; finally, he was mostly interested in sex. Ann was compassionate toward him, then annoyed, then angry.

She talked to his wife and to any other lovers he had had, then reversed roles with each of them.

She found someone else and was happy; she had a hard

time meeting someone; she never found anyone as "good" as Bill.

She talked to friends and found them supportive, then annoyed with her, then angry. She reversed roles with them.

Just thinking about confronting Bill brought on an arousal response in Ann, which increased her anxieties. To help herself, she pictured scenes related to her body's reaction to her fears, imagining feeling her heart rate accelerate a little and her breathing quicken and originate from her chest. She imagined experiencing normal arousal due to her fears of losing Bill, then experiencing more intense arousal. She continually reaffirmed that these were her body's protective mechanisms (described in Chapter Seven).

Now she imagined having difficulty with her heart and breathing; consulting a physician who reassured her, then recommended a tranquilizer. She reversed roles with the doctor. She imagined her throat tightening, then loosening; all her arousal responses acting to help her fend off an attack, then that she had difficulty getting control of her breathing back; going to an emergency room, playing the roles of patient, doctor, and supportive friends.

Ann continued getting angry at herself for being afraid of her body, then being supportive for its quick response to any threat; provoking the arousal response with fears of losing Bill, then calming herself down to show her control; discussing the arousal response with a doctor, on an academic level, as a frightened patient, as the doctor reassuring a patient.

As her skill with imagery increased, Ann progressed to more difficult scenes: telling her friends and family about Bill, first sympathetically, then neutrally and finally negatively; her friends responding with support, then shock, then anger.

In her scenes, Ann imagined being awkward, then embarrassed, and finally humiliated as she recounted her affair to friends. She pictured them reversing roles with her. She tried scenes with a new lover, with sexual problems, with a fear of intimacy. She imagined that her friends and family rejected her, then that Bill did. She pictured living with him, being married to him, the anxieties about his honesty, fidelity, and responsibility.

As she gradually became desensitized to her anxieties, Ann's fears changed dramatically. When she saw him at work, she no longer had difficulty withstanding his annoyance, because she was prepared by her imagery. That, coupled with her lack of fear, sent a message of confidence and assertiveness, which had an intimidating effect on Bill.

Therapy also helped Ann to recognize that she had been thinking about leaving Bill almost from the start. The thought of it not working out had often crossed her mind and continued to worry her. She tried to distract herself with work and exercise, but when her mind was free to wander, concerns about Bill's intentions floated to the surface. Ann learned to allow herself to consider the possibilities, becoming aware that the mind sets a high priority on survival issues and that the process provides emotional desensitization so she could handle problems.

She set aside time during the day to use imagery and confront her fears. Typically, early morning walks and after dinner were the best times for her. If fears and anxieties intruded at other times of the day, she promised herself time to think through them later as necessary, so she could do her work.

When the final split came, Ann was better prepared than she expected. She had sleepless nights and fits of anguish, but they came sporadically. She had done most of the grief work, dealing with loss, while she was still with Bill. As a result, she was able to resume a social life much earlier than she expected, avoiding the contamination of future relationships by endlessly rehashing her problems with Bill.

Once she was free of her relationship with Bill, Ann was also free to recognize her anger: at herself for being manipulated by him; at him for his lies and deception; and in general for the time lost and the grief experienced. Confronting Bill and letting him know her feelings alleviated some of her anger. Ann considered and rejected revenge against Bill's family as compensation but realized she would never make up the time and pain he had caused her.

To help herself, Ann enrolled in a night college program to get a CPA certificate. She took guitar lessons and promised herself she would find a lover who appreciated her qualities. To compensate her family and friends, she offered more interest and attention, including monthly dinners and attendance at all family parties. She expanded her social life, meeting friends after work, going out with coworkers, seeing her relatives regularly. Ann remarked she would not have thought of paying herself back so comprehensively, but it was helping her overcome her anger. She was happy and having fun, looking forward, not backward.

The affair with Bill had some long-term implications. Ann committed herself to making restitution to herself, friends, and family for her mistakes and strengthening her own character. The relationship with Bill had reflected her tendency to find a quick fix for problems. Other areas of her life also provided evidence of how her impatience and impulsive actions often worked to her detriment. As she became more aware of her penchant to act before she examined the situation, she tried to be more reflective and more considerate of advice from others.

Another bad trait was her willingness to relinquish control of her life to someone like Bill. Ann often got pleasure and reassurance from helping others, even to her own disadvantage. She decided to cut back her savior and rescue missions, realizing that some people repaid kindness by taking advantage of it.

Sandi and the Mood Swinger

It took Sandi years to get over her husband's death when she was forty-two. They had a wonderful marriage and two children, and she was devastated when she lost him to cancer.

She had never had a job, and at first she worried about how she could support her family. But she learned to work with a computer and got a clerical job, working her way up to office manager.

Two years after Sandi became a widow, she lost a friend to ovarian cancer. Shortly after the funeral, Stan, the new widower, asked her out. They dated for two years before getting married. Throughout the courtship, he doted on her, buying her cards and flowers and complimenting everything she did. Stan professed great love for Sandi, but she realized later that she never really loved him. She remembered being fond of him and developing a close attachment to him.

While they were dating, Stan drank in moderation and never expressed anger or even irritation. He always seemed to be in a good mood, working hard but spending freely.

After they were married, he began to change. His drinking increased steadily and he became irritable over trivial things. He got furious whenever he misplaced something and usually blamed Sandi. Stan was spending more and more time in front of the television and less and less time socializing.

The phone never rang anymore because most of her friends didn't like her husband. Stan hated the two-hour trip to visit Sandi's parents, so they stopped seeing them. Sandi felt trapped, with nowhere to go and no one to visit. She tried talking about it, but Stan blamed her indirectly. He had to work hard to pay their bills since she had only a part-time job. He wasn't in the mood to extend himself.

Things got worse, mostly because of Stan's drinking. He lost his job and began spending more time alone. He was frequently nasty, argumentative, and accusative, criticizing Sandi for everything from rearranging his "things" when she cleaned house to spending too much money.

He blew up over minor things, Sandi's "overcautious" driving, for example, then apologized and begged for forgiveness. Stan blamed Sandi for his bad moods, stretching logic to make his argument. She wondered if she were going crazy.

Then he accused her of having an affair with the dentist, making a fool of the dentist and humiliating Sandi. Within minutes, he was apologizing again, blaming his outburst on alcohol.

Sandi saw a lawyer, who advised her to leave, predicting that Stan would hit her. That night he did, although he didn't know she had been warned. Sandi returned to the lawyer for a divorce and on his recommendation also came in for therapy.

To begin, Sandi learned to recognize the characteristics of mood swingers and to see how closely Stan's behavior followed the pattern. From the start he was insecure about their relationship, convinced that other men wanted his beautiful, wonderful wife. But his early behavior was unexceptional and contained until he felt secure enough to free his moods. He denied and tried to hide his mood swings, blaming emotional changes on someone else's behavior, confusing the real cause.

The gradual pattern was accelerated by the stress of unemployment. To (temporarily) reduce his insecurity, he tried to control Sandi, using lies and manipulation to maintain the control. Finally he turned to alcohol, and then to violence.

For the next step, Sandi identified the bonds between them, acknowledging too few of the feelings that keep two people together existed in their relationship. She had some degree of care, concern, and fidelity. She did want him to get better (psychological bonds). They ate dinner together, shared chores at home, and occasionally went shopping (behavioral bonds). But the emotional bonds were all negative: She feared his moods, his potential for violence, his refusal to let her go, his threats if she left. She also had a great deal of anger toward him, especially when he was sober.

To break the psychological bonds, Sandi looked closely at Stan's behavior and recognized the characteristics of a mood swinger and abuser. She had tried several times to get Stan to accept help. He rejected therapy and AA and denied the concerns of friends and family. Not even the physical problems that developed from his heavy drinking prompted him to give up the bottle or his other self-destructive habits. She realized at last that he would not change and that continuing their marriage was futile.

Like many other people, Sandi knew the relationship was impossible, but she was afraid to take the next step and leave, even though she recognized how potentially dangerous it was to continue living with Stan. A support group helped Sandi recognize how typical Stan's behavior and attitudes were. Even a lawyer who had never met Stan was able to predict the violence that followed.

It also became clear that Sandi, too, was feeling the effects of Stan's behavior in many ways. Her health was worsening and her self-esteem was declining. She was depressed and isolated. She had no control over her life, no growth or development.

If anything, her personality was deteriorating, developing passive-aggressive tendencies to oppose Stan. She sabotaged her own self-image to avoid confronting him. Her children, almost grown, were also suffering. Stan's problems took priority; fear of his anger and moodiness caused them physical problems, and Sandi's passivity left them without a role model.

Once these things became clear, Sandi filed for divorce and got a restraining order barring Stan from the house. Eventually she moved out. She practiced being more assertive and selective with her companions. Those actions broke the behavioral bonds, but Sandi also had to work on her emotional ties to Stan.

Like Ann, Sandi used imagery to confront Stan about his petty accusations, his threats, and his drinking. She role-played his responses, rehearsing what she would say in every imaginable scenario, including violence. She also imagined talking to her friends and family about Stan's drinking, her sense of shame for staying with him so long, and her guilt about neglecting the other people in her life because of his intractable problems.

At first, Sandi claimed to be overwhelmed with guilt at the thought of confronting Stan. Hurting him, despite what he had done to her, seemed unbearable. She felt she could never hurt anyone.

Eventually, through therapy, she acknowledged that by not letting Stan know how she felt about him she was, in fact, hurting him. She was also hurting her children by staying in the marriage, hurting herself, and hurting her family and friends by avoiding them to appease Stan. She realized that it was her inability to deal with her fears of confronting Stan, not her unwillingness to hurt people, that brought on her accommodating behavior.

To meet those fears, Sandi imagined trying to make things work with Stan, loving him, hating him, being with him. She pictured what would happen if her love could rescue him, how proud she would feel. Her images ranged from blissful scenes to real anguish. She thought about the good as well as the bad in their marriage, his loving courtship as well as his destructive drinking.

Long walks helped Sandi face her fears. She repeatedly summoned up the images and vigorously confronted them. She wanted to speed up the emotional desensitization of her fears as well as her residual feelings for Stan so she could get on with her life. She worked hard at it, spending time on issues related to violence and emergency preparations. Her depression came not so much from losing Stan as from her recognition that she had lost time, opportunity, friends, and personal growth.

As a result, Sandi was angrier with herself than with Stan. She pitied him, seeing him as a hopeless alcoholic and abuser. To get relief from her anger, she worked out compensation for herself that included both presents and a future. Sandi committed herself to revamping her life, taking advanced courses on the computer, joining a spa, and buying herself two Lhasa apsos, pedigreed dogs she had always wanted.

She found she had more peace by forgiving Stan, not taking revenge. Sandi also learned to acknowledge her own personality faults that had created some of the problem, resolving to work on improving her character, expressing her assertiveness, and abandoning her need to be a rescuer.

Linda and the Perpetual Adolescent

A CPA and MBA, thirty-six-year-old Linda had a good job with a large accounting firm, but her professional success was not duplicated in her personal life, although she was attractive and self-confident. When Dave joined her firm, he quickly became the office stud. He was only two years younger than she, and Linda found him very attractive. She liked his tight, lean physique, his personality, and his charm. She tried a few subtle approaches, but when he didn't respond, she decided her interest wasn't returned.

Then Dave asked her out for a drink after work. Soon they were going out together on weekends, and things were terrific. For a few months, all was well, then Dave began acting irresponsibly. He would make plans to meet Linda for breakfast or dinner and cancel at the last minute. Linda was humiliated but hesitated to confront him about it. She noticed that he would gradually show more interest in her, then spoil it by inappropriately teasing her about frumpy clothes or her conservative opinions.

Linda tried to talk to Dave about his erratic interest and odd behavior, but he denied everything. When his antics continued, she became discouraged, lost hope, and withdrew her feelings. He seemed to sense her coolness and asked her about it, but Linda remained aloof. He changed jobs shortly after and disappeared from her life.

A year later, Dave called and invited her out for a drink. Curious, Linda accepted, marveling at how casual he was about the twelve-month gap in their relationship. It was as if there had been no break and nothing had changed. Linda decided to go along for the ride, and they started dating again. At first, he seemed more responsible, committed to an exercise regime and long-distance running. Within months, the old habits emerged. When the cycle of interest and disinterest began, Linda decided to seek therapy.

Despite herself, she had fallen deeply in love with Dave. She recognized that a long-term commitment from him was futile, so she sought help. First, Linda learned how closely Dave's behavior followed the characteristics for the adolescent personality type.

Dave was charming, intriguing, appealing, and challenging at first. The destructive behavior emerged slowly.

He had no interest in developing a relationship or sharing a life with Linda or anyone. He wanted to keep his independence and freedom. To maintain control of the relationship, he was manipulative, insensitive, and deceitful.

Dave became interested when Linda pulled away, then lost interest when she wanted more, keeping her off balance and the relationship from growing. Predictably, Linda was stressed, developing gastrointestinal disorders, insomnia, generalized anxiety, low self-esteem, grief over her anticipated loss, and anger at herself for being drawn into his orbit a second time.

Linda began by identifying the bonds that tied her to Dave. Psychological bonds included her care and concern for him, and her attachment, fidelity, and affection. The behavioral ones included dining, sex, jogging, dancing, spending time together. The emotional ties were her love, her anxiety over the relationship, her fear of losing him, her fears of rejection and abandonment, and her depression due to the futility of the affair.

Recognizing Dave's behavior as abusive and characteristic of perpetual adolescents, Linda realized how controlling, manipulative, deceitful, and immature he was. Self-centered and inaccessible, he had no interest in changing and no concern for Linda's needs. Her attempts to get him to alter his behavior and work on the relationship were useless, further severing her psychological tie to Dave. Again, therapy helped by pointing out how predictable his behavior was and how typical their relationship had been.

Linda also came to see the destructive effect the affair had had on her, both emotionally and physically. She began to feel a great deal of anger toward herself for not ending the situation sooner.

To break the emotional bonds, Linda began working on her fears through imagery. She gave herself permission to confront each of her fears. She imagined that the relationship reached a peak and then Dave disappeared again. She asked Dave to explain his behavior, then confronted him, argued with him, and finally told him off. She role-played his position, then switched back to her position.

She imagined losing him. She imagined marrying him, which brought out new fears of living with doubt about the solidity of the relationship. She imagined his good points as well as the bad ones.

Throughout the imaging, Linda experienced the physical symptoms of an arousal reaction under the worst of circumstances. But she gained control of them.

For her feelings of depression, Linda had to work on her need to see Dave after she broke off their affair. He was always willing to make a date, so she had to control her urge to call him or accept his infrequent calls. She used imagery here, too, imagining that she called Dave and they had an enjoyable time together. At first this triggered her interest, but gradually she became desensitized.

Then she imagined the details of an entire day with him, including sex. She returned to this image over and over until she grew bored with it. She imagined him as kind and caring as well as manipulative and deceitful.

Gradually, her urge to see him grew less intense. She did meet him a few more times, but her view of him as unsuitable was reinforced even though they enjoyed each other's company. Each time, he acted as if nothing had happened, as if they were just picking up their old relationship where it had left off. He was too quick to forget, but this time Linda was prepared and impervious to his manipulations.

Most of Linda's anger was directed toward herself, not Dave. She didn't see the point of getting back at him; she just wanted to get on with her life. Standing up for herself wouldn't change Dave, and the relationship was over. She didn't want him to think she was still interested or even cared enough to still be angry.

Instead, she decided to help herself, to take on exercise, diet, and other programs to feel better about herself. To make up for her lost time opportunity, and growth, she promised to treat herself better. She opened her own CPA practice, giving her more control over her life and expanding her social contacts. It also provided her with more exposure to men in general, something her fear of rejection had limited in the past. She tried to be more careful about the men in her life but also to remember that most men are not like Dave.

Jane and the Controller

When Jane began therapy, she had a problem I'd heard many times before. She had been married to Bob for nearly two years. At thirty, Jane was attractive, well dressed, and interesting. She worked as a real estate broker and management consultant, earning enough to live comfortably. Bob was more ambitious. Only a year older, he was the vice president of a real estate company and earned more than $100,000 a year. He was very competitive, especially in his amateur basketball and softball leagues, but was well liked by everyone. He had a great sense of humor, was sensitive to others, and generous to a fault.

The more Jane talked, the better Bob sounded. He loved her and was very attentive, considering her needs and trying to please her. He talked of Jane as his best friend and spent most of his free time with her. She was an equal in the relationship, consulted on every decision with differences negotiated between them. They almost never argued and had only one area of disagreement. Bob was Mr. Wonderful—except for his mother. (I hear that same phrase all the time, with different endings: ". . . except he smokes, he has AIDS, he can't hold a job, he drinks . . ." The range of possibilities is infinite.)

Almost every Sunday, Jane and Bob visited his parents, usually staying for dinner. Emily, Bob's mother, ruled the house, allowing her husband little say in most matters. She never demanded Bob's presence but was quick to make him feel guilty if he missed a weekend. Domineering and forceful, Emily was very attached to Bob, and he, in turn, seemed blind to her manipulations.

Emily was coolly friendly toward her daughter-in-law, but Jane knew Emily really didn't like her. The older woman used snide remarks and subtle comments to belittle Jane. Emily offered suggestions on how Jane should fix up the apartment, jokingly commenting that Jane was more interested in fashion than cooking. One day, she remarked, "God bless these girls today who can't cook or clean. I don't know how they keep a man."

An assertive woman used to speaking her mind, Jane tried to bite her tongue when her mother-in-law sounded off. When she did snap a reply, Bob became upset and argued with her for the rest of the evening. Jane tried to explain her feelings to Bob, but he refused to listen. He just said Jane was overreacting and should try harder to get along with his mother. After hours of discussion, Jane said the weekly visits were unbearable to her. She wanted to reduce the frequency or let him visit his family without her. Bob insisted that she come along.

Not sure if she was exaggerating the situation, Jane discussed it with her friends ad nauseam. By now they were all tired of hearing about Emily and Bob, and Jane felt guilty if she brought the issue up. Her parents thought Bob was incapable of standing up to his mother and Jane should leave him.

When Jane came in for therapy, I was concerned about the accuracy of Jane's perception of Emily's hostility. I had seen insecure women so in need of reassurance and support from their husbands that they set up situations where he would have to choose her over his mother. They often also tried to make their husbands more dependent on them, further alienating the men from their mothers.

But that didn't seem to be the situation between Jane and Emily. Jane was a strong, assertive woman who felt confident of her partner. She didn't need to alienate Bob from his mother or make him dependent on her. Jane had tried to get along with Bob's mother but found her accommodations greeted with escalating nastiness and disrespect. Her attempts to keep the peace had backfired.

Although Bob seemed to be independent and assertive in most areas of his life, he was overly attached to and dependent on his mother. He had a need to control the interaction between Jane and Emily. When they disagreed, Bob would intervene, enforcing a superficial cease-fire between the women. If Jane responded to Emily's insults, Bob argued with her or stopped speaking to her for days. Jane felt she was given a choice: endure Emily's insults or Bob's anger.

Bob was too insecure and nonassertive with his mother to see Jane's point of view. He wanted only compliance from Jane on the issue and refused to try to understand or support her position. Jane bought temporary peace by stifling her reaction to Emily, but the weekly visits were torture. She felt abused and degraded at the family dinners.

Jane began to realize that by accommodating Emily she was enabling Bob to control the situation. She also noticed some parallels between Bob's relationship with his mother and with her. Both were strong women, but Emily was very controlled around Bob. She never snapped at him and seemed cautious. It was obvious that she feared he would visit less frequently if she upset him.

It was similar to the arrangement he had tried to work out with Jane—go along with the visit and you won't get punished. Emily feared that if she got him angry, he wouldn't visit. Jane was afraid that if she antagonized him, he would leave her. As a result, she didn't press her arguments about his mother. She tried to get Bob to speak to Emily, but he balked, saying it was Jane's responsibility to get along with her. He wouldn't discuss it further and refused to acknowledge Emily's role. Jane felt trapped, faced with an insoluble problem.

Jane began to recognize that Bob's behavior was following the pattern of the controller. He used control to conceal his insecurity. All rules and decisions were made unilaterally. If Jane questioned his control, he lost his temper, using anger to punish Jane.

Bob was inflexible and showed no respect for Jane's feelings or point of view. He rejected criticism, insisting that whatever was bothering Jane was her fault. Nothing was open for discussion.

When Jane began working with imagery to reduce her anxiety and her fears of confronting Bob, she began with easy scenes. First she asked Bob's opinion on how to deal with his mother. Then she imagined asking him how to handle the veiled insults she got from Emily, for example, when Emily invited Bob for Thanksgiving, then asked if he was bringing Jane. Finally she imagined telling Bob that she believed Emily saw their marriage as a threat to her mother-son relationship.

She discussed her feelings of hurt by Emily's coldness and talked about Bob's refusal to listen to her. She offered her point of view and imagined his usual responses: "I don't want to discuss it," "You should just get along with her," "Don't argue over everything." Jane imagined getting angry at Bob, accusing him of being controlling, then voicing her opinion of his relationship with Emily.

After a while, Jane was able to imagine Bob saying he was leaving her and what it would be like to lose him, live alone, find someone new, and tell her friends she'd been rejected.

With practice, Jane gradually desensitized herself to her fears of confronting Bob and even of losing him. She allowed herself to feel the arousal response. As she manipulated the images, she noticed the effect on the feelings of arousal and she practiced controlling her fears by varying the images. She also worked on controlling her breathing to reduce her feelings of anxiety. Soon she had progressed to more complex and difficult images, dealing with related problems, such as discussing the problems with her family and friends, and their reactions, from annoyance to shock to anger to support.

Then she reversed roles with Bob, imagining how he would respond to her different approaches. She even tried imagery with Emily.

As she became less threatened and more confident, Jane told Bob that she wanted to discuss her feelings about the situation with Emily. At first Bob refused and became irritable, but Jane wasn't intimidated and pushed him to respond. She was prepared for his response and no longer feared losing him. She had recognized that she could not ignore the problem or allow herself to be controlled by Bob.

When Jane insisted on the discussion, Bob refused to listen to her point of view and wouldn't discuss the matter at all. He resorted to ridiculing her and repeatedly threatened her with "take it or leave it" ultimatums. When that didn't work, he seemed ready to listen, but Jane didn't think he was really sincere. He apparently realized she wasn't going to back down and said whatever he had in order to get peace. Although he promised to talk to Emily, he never did. And although he promised to support Jane if she was right and unfairly criticized, he never followed up on that either.

Gradually Jane realized that Bob had to have control. It was only in one area now, with his mother, but the pattern would recur. Jane decided to end the marriage, explaining, "It will get worse, and much worse if we have children." Once she was away from him, she could see more clearly that there had been other signs that Bob was a controller, such as isolating her from her friends and family. It was her fear that without Bob she would never have children that blinded her to his manipulations, she realized.

As Jane examined the psychological bonds with Bob, she realized that she no longer trusted him. She doubted her loyalty to him and his to her. She felt no commitment from him if he wasn't interested in defending her when she was attacked. There were other values, like respect for each other's feelings, that they didn't share, and he was more concerned with control than he was about her.

They did have many behavioral bonds—tennis, dining out, movies, vacations, shared chores, visiting his parents, and living together. But Jane reestablished her relations with her own friends and family. She took steps to meet people, enrolling in a spa, joining a local tennis club, and going out with friends whenever possible.

In a fairly short time, Jane met Peter. He shared her interests in movies and sports and also worked in real estate. They had a lot of common values, and Peter didn't have feelings of inadequacy that fostered a need for control and rigidity. As she thought about it, she and Peter shared psychological bonds of trust, affiliation, commitment, loyalty, care, concern, and honesty. They enjoyed doing things together from sports and work to visiting family and friends. And they had many emotional bonds: sexual attraction, love, shared feelings of contentment, and attachment. Theirs was a relationship of equals with regard to power and control, fluid enough to respond to new circumstances and situations.

*   *   *

Ann, Sandi, Linda, and Jane each faced up to a series of fears about life without the man who had been the focus of recent years. Imagery helped each woman confront anxieties about living alone, friends, family, new situations, and future responses to another man.

In each case, the treatment was basically the same:

1. Recognize the problem behavior pattern.
2. Identify the specific emotional, behavioral, and psychological bonds in your relationship.
3. Examine the mate's behavior and concern for your needs with regard to those bonds.
4. Use imagery to confront fears about ending the relationship and all related issues.
5. Develop a strategy to compensate for past lies, manipulations, abuse, pain, and anguish as well as current anger.
6. Work on changing personal character traits that attract you to impossible people.
7. Expand support groups, family contacts, social activities.
8. Develop new interests, take courses, travel.

If you follow these steps, taking them gradually and changing the images if you get too upset, you can help yourself to fall out of love. And by understanding what happened in the relationship, how to escape, and how to regain your self-esteem, you will land on your feet.